Squirrels, Boats,

and

Thoroughbreds

JAMIE GERDSEN

Squirrels, Boats,

and

Thoroughbreds

LESSONS *for* LEADING CHANGE
in TRADITIONAL BUSINESSES

RIVER GROVE
BOOKS

Published by River Grove Books
Austin, TX
www.greenleafbookgroup.com

Copyright ©2013 Jamie Gerdsen

All rights reserved.

No part of this book may be reproduced, stored in a retrieval system, or transmitted by any means, electronic, mechanical, photocopying, recording, or otherwise, without written permission from the copyright holder.

Distributed by River Grove Books

For ordering information or special discounts for bulk purchases, please contact River Grove Books at PO Box 91869, Austin, TX 78709, 512.891.6100.

Design and composition by Greenleaf Book Group LLC
Cover design by Greenleaf Book Group LLC

Cataloging-in-Publication data
(Prepared by The Donohue Group, Inc.)

Gerdsen, Jamie.
    Squirrels, boats, and thoroughbreds : lessons for leading change in traditional businesses / Jamie Gerdsen.—1st ed.
    p. ; cm.
    Issued also as an ebook.
    ISBN-13: 978-1-938416-30-9 (hardbound)
    ISBN-10: 1-938416-30-9 (hardbound)
    ISBN-13: 978-1-938416-31-6 (softbound)
    ISBN-10: 1-938416-31-7 (softbound)
    ISBN-13: 978-1-938416-32-3 (eBook)
    1. Organizational change. 2. Leadership. 3. Industrial management. 4. Personnel management. I. Title.

HD58.8 .G47 2013
658.4/06   2013936757

First Edition

I would like to dedicate this to all those who have been told they can't but do.

I would like to acknowledge my family. None of what I have written would have been possible without your unconditional support through all the challenges. And to my boys, Jack and Pete, you are the legacy of my hard work and love.

Contents

You live out loud,

You laugh, you hope,

You like to push the envelope.

You know your song by heart and sing it.

Life gets tough and you say

Bring it.

Words I Live By—J.G.

1

Call to Action

It was a doozy of a wake-up call.

I was working in sales at a Tampa-based telecommunications company. My boss—a nice guy who had been with the company only a few months and had just relocated his family from the Northeast—was fired by fax. That's right, by fax. Can you believe that? No spanking session in the corner office. No obligatory sit-down session with HR. No "Sorry it didn't work out," "The company has hit a rough patch," or "We're consolidating divisions and there wasn't a spot for you."

Just *poof*. You're gone.

I'd joined this company when it was a start-up and witnessed its transformation to a corporation interested only in maximizing income. It was sort of the corporate version of Jekyll turning into Hyde. It was no longer a culture in which I wanted to work. If they would fire my boss by fax, they could fire me the same way.

I left that very day.

That was the first smart thing I did. The second was to go to work with my dad at Apollo Heating and Air Conditioning.

Not that everybody at Apollo was pleased to learn I'd be joining the company. When I showed up that first day, nobody liked me. In fact, one staffer actually said, "It's over. In five years, the place will be out of business."

I know what you're thinking—as the son of the owner—I'd probably been given some cushy job. Say VP of Marketing or Executive Vice President with a starting salary in the low six figures. Well, you'd be wrong.

I wanted to work with my dad because we'd always had a great relationship. But I didn't want to live off my dad. I wanted to make it on my own. So I started as a sales guy totally on commission. I only earned when I sold.

Some people told me that was crazy. I like to think it was the third smart thing I did: I gave myself adversity to overcome knowing that I'd work harder rowing against the current.

It worked. I worked, like the proverbial government mule. I had a half-million dollars more in sales than the next leading salesman. I sold things the other salesmen couldn't. I beat every sales quota on Apollo's books. I had to. I had a family to support.

About that five years and the company will be history comment: It's now been ten years and the company is thriving. I give my dad much of the credit for that. But I give myself a little, too. I bought the company from him three years ago, and since then we've grown exponentially.

It's interesting to me that all you hear these days in the way of business success stories are ones about dot com start-ups, e-tailers, or social media outlets. But there's success to be had with more traditional businesses. Like mine. And potentially yours.

What I had to do—and what you'll have to do if you're in charge of leading a traditional business—is separate sound thinking from conventional thinking. One leads to success. The other merely continues the status quo. This book endeavors to move you into the realm of sound thinkers.

You see, much of the advice I received as a young entrepreneur was conventional. I learned the hard way that conventional thinking seldom produces results. It was only after I shifted to sound thinking that Apollo began its run of exponential growth.

"Smart is the new rich," a leading financial pundit announced the other night on his syndicated TV show. I believe him. I'm not rich; not yet at least. But I'm going to be. Rowing against the current smartened me up. What I learned, I'm happy to share. My hope is that this book will make you smarter, and if the pundit is right, that's going to make you richer.

What Success Feels Like

Most businesspeople don't know what success feels like. They often describe success as making a pot of money, enough to buy all sorts of fancy adult toys. To many, nothing says success like a yellow Lamborghini parked in his or her reserved CEO space. Other less-materialistic executives describe success as a destination, the end of a hard-fought journey. They say, "When I get there, I'll know it."

I was fortunate. I got a taste of success at a very early age. And perhaps because no one expected me to achieve it, it tasted all that much sweeter.

As a child, I was diagnosed with a learning disability. Maybe I had one. Maybe I didn't. Either way, school never came easily to me. But just being labeled with something like that affects you. It becomes a self-fulfilling prophecy. The fact that I was big for my age only compounded the problem. It snowballed. Big *and* dumb.

During my freshman year in high school I discovered competitive rowing, and it transformed my life. I'd finally found something at which I was really good. I was part of a four-man team that competed at nationals that year. It was a little bit like the movie *Hoosiers*. We were the team no one expected to do anything, and yet we finished a respectable fourth. I was hooked.

My sophomore year, we had a new coach and better equipment—an eight-man rowing shell. Practices were physically draining. I worked harder than I'd ever worked in my life. By nationals, the team was strong and in sync.

Nationals that year were in Indianapolis, a place I hadn't rowed before. During the heats, we did not have good rows, and our coach called us out on it. He knew we all thought we were just a small-town team and that we might not belong on the national stage. He changed all that the night before the final.

He had us visualize the race second by second, minute by minute. The race itself would last a mere six minutes, but during the visualization process, he took us from launch to finish. He had us start by visualizing putting our hands on the boat in preparation for launch, then the warm-ups, and finally the sprint from the starting line to the finish.

On race day, the events up to the start were just how we visualized them. As we pulled up to the start, my heart felt like it was going to come through my chest. We sat, waiting, for a long moment of pin-drop silence. *Boom* the 2,000-meter race was on. At the 1,000-meter point we were in fifth place. My hopes of winning were fading quickly until our coxswain called a "power 20." That's twenty strokes as hard as you can do them. I closed my eyes and lost myself in putting everything I had into each stroke. With about 200 meters to go, I opening my eyes as the coxswain called out twenty strokes to the finish.

We won the USRowing Youth National Championship by four seconds. It was a glorious feeling, my first taste of success. And, oh, how I savored it.

Many times during the early days at Apollo I called on that experience for motivation.

As a commission sales guy, I was driving from customer home to customer home in my 1991 burgundy Saturn with its beige interior and over 130,000 miles on the odometer. I'd finish the call, only to find my car—parked in the prospect's driveway—had a dead battery. How embarrassing to have to go back, ring the doorbell, and ask the prospect for a jump. Ugh. I took comfort that this was like rowing practice in the rain. The tougher it goes, the stronger it makes you.

Just like rowing, I committed totally to selling. No distractions. No slacking off. I ran my calls, spending as much time as needed to make sure a prospect felt good about Apollo. I returned after the installation to make sure prospects—now customers—were happy with the work. If they weren't, I made sure it was made right.

I worked constantly to make the installers and the service techs know we were teammates. I wanted to make them the best they could be, because I knew that would help me be successful.

And last, I applied my own visualization. I pictured myself being successful at sales, and I began envisioning what my next steps at Apollo might be.

Success, I discovered, can have many facets. When I first arrived at Apollo, success was earning enough in commissions to put food on the table. (I used to jokingly say I could starve with the best of them.) When my sales efforts took off, success became understanding the intricate runnings of the business, and still later, success became putting the new leadership team in place.

My point is that success changes. It's like a video game. You reach one level only to realize you have a new challenge in reaching the next. Savor each level as you complete it, and relish the challenge of the next. Never become satisfied. That's the kiss of death.

I had a friend who was driven to make his company the premier one in his region. He worked tirelessly. Did whatever it took. Made the investment back in the company to fund growth.

Over a period of five years, he did it. In fact, he did it so well his trade association honored him with a dinner and big plaque of achievement. In my mind I can still see him holding it high over his head and grinning. It was the beginning of the end.

He'd tasted success. He'd reached his goal. Unfortunately, because he didn't have other goals and never adjusted his goal upward, his company began to wither away. Within three years, it was a shell of its former self. Only the plaque remained as a reminder of the glory days.

This doesn't have to happen. As you grow, set new goals. Think both vertically and horizontally. You can grow your core business—vertical growth. Or you can add ancillary businesses—horizontal growth—that allow you to diversify and potentially extend into new markets.

Consumer goods companies, like Procter & Gamble, are

constantly readjusting their portfolios and adding line extensions to their most profitable brands. We can all learn from what companies like P&G, Apple, and Google are doing. They're never content. They visualize growth both vertically and horizontally, and because they're big companies, they have the resources to make that growth happen.

LOOK AHEAD

❏ Visualize your own success. Once you have, commit it to writing so that you have a record. Journaling your thoughts will help make your visualization and subsequent ideas tangible. I've journaled the events in my life for years. I even took it a step further and have each year's written pages professionally bound together in leather.

❏ Now that you've visualized success, begin to list the things you need to do to make that success a reality. This can be behavior modification, financial investment, trying something new, and so on. Make this list as complete as you possibly can.

❏ Now that you have a list of actions you need to take for success, put a timetable and action plan together to make each one happen. Remember, success usually doesn't come from one big thing. It happens by doing a number of smaller things. Start by working your way down your list of action items one at a time. As you accomplish each one, give yourself a pat on the back. You've earned it. You're a step closer to success.

See Your Future

Visualization is a powerful, time-tested tool. My rowing coach was tapping into a long sports tradition of visualization to help our team realize we could win the nationals. Others use visualization, too. Here is a list of examples:

- Hitters visualize what they'll be thrown by the pitcher.
- Closers visualize the final inning and see getting that final out.
- Quarterbacks visualize where their wide receivers will be on the field and see the throw being completed.
- Business executives visualize a key meeting—noting the white knights, black knights, and shape shifters at the table— and anticipate their comments and concerns.
- Speakers visualize the room, the audience, and the podium from which they'll be orating. They see themselves confidently delivering their speech.

- Orchestra musicians visualize their performance and hear the selections being played.

- Architects visualize how buildings might look long before they ever begin to draw plans.

These days, a whole industry has grown up around visualization. There are facilitators who will assist your company in developing growth scenarios. Marketing firms offer ideation sessions. Futurists predict consumer trends and offer insight into the products and trends that will be hot in the marketplace.

So why has visualization gotten to be such a big deal? Just as individuals can use it to increase performance, businesses can use it to see their future. Think of it this way. There's a saying, "Any road will get you there if you don't know where you're going." Visualization allows your organization to know where it's going so that you find the right road to get you there.

Visualization can be one of your best competitive advantages. By visualizing how your industry is changing and what future customers will demand from it, you can position your company in the best place to satisfy those consumers.

This isn't just crystal ball gazing, either. You can use visualization to see how an added service might impact the organization, what increased staffing levels might offer, how cost cutting might impact service, how a different shop layout might speed workflow, what an added location would generate in additional customers. The list goes on and on.

How do you use visualization? You'll find it's surprisingly easy.

To make the most productive use of your time, there are some guidelines you should follow:

- **Choose the subject of your visualization.** Using ourselves as an example, we might visualize how the organization would function if we added electric to HVAC and plumbing. Make your visualization topic specific. Otherwise, you'll be blue-skying everything and anything. Setting parameters works to your benefit.

- **Decide who should participate in the visualization.** Smaller groups work best; anything over ten people is too many. Five people make an ideal group size. Don't automatically choose the five people at the top. You'd like to have a diversity of viewpoints. I always like to have someone from sales in the group because that person is closest to the customer.

- **Don't be afraid to include someone from outside the company.** Sometimes having an objective outside viewpoint is very advantageous. If there's a subject expert, an accountant or lawyer who would add value to the discussion, invite that person to join you. Outsiders are usually respectfully quiet at the start. Make it a point to engage them in the conversation and get them actively involved.

- **Consider an off-site location.** This visualization is important, and if you hold it in your conference room, someone will be sticking his or her head in the door every five minutes for some reason or other that he or she deems important. Those interruptions disrupt the process and hurt productivity.

Don't limit yourself in that way. Go off-site where you'll have the group's full attention.

- **Tell the group what you'll be doing**. If the purpose of the session is to talk about what the company might look like after the addition of electric, share that in advance as the task to be accomplished. Head off any speculation as to what this is about, and don't make them guess what they'll be doing.

- **Leave titles at the door**. If everyone is waiting to hear what the boss says before speaking, your session is doomed. Make a point of telling everyone that there is no rank in the room. Everyone is equal. All comments carry the same weight.

- **Assign homework prior to the visualization**. You'll want to make sure the appropriate people at the table have brought all the facts and figures needed to aid your discussions. Don't be caught wanting some needed piece of information.

- **Designate a scribe**. Paper the walls and appoint someone to capture the comments of the group on those sheets so that the group visually has the benefit of what's been said. This visual flow of the meeting will keep things moving forward and keep you from revisiting old ground.

- **Capture verbatims**. Use a recording device to capture all comments from the group. Have this transcribed so that you have a complete written record.

- **Try to put your conclusions or results in visual form**. Most of us are visual interpreters. By putting your results in schematic form, you have a better chance of having everyone truly understand the group's conclusions.

- **Have a parking lot.** There will be intriguing ideas that come up but are off topic. Designate one sheet as a "parking lot." List the intriguing off-topic ideas on it for consideration at a different session. *Warning*: Parking lot items often get forgotten. If a particularly intriguing item comes up, don't risk losing it. Put someone in charge of scheduling a visualization to flesh out that item.

- **Assign follow-up.** If there are areas that could use further research or study, assign tasks and have the additional information that is generated circulated to the group.

- **Gain consensus on what has been achieved.** Don't end the meeting until there is a summation of what the group has accomplished. Make sure everyone feels his or her voice has been heard. Only then can you truly move forward as a unified group. It's important that everyone have buy-in to the final recommendations.

Remember, a visualization session is a tool. Take a hammer, for example. Properly used, you'll drive home the needed nails. But you can also smack your thumb. Visualization can give you a valuable look at the future, but it can easily turn into a bitch session. Keep it positive. Keep it on-point. And keep it tactile.

My rowing coach sure did. He described things in such detail that it made it easy for us to conjure up the right images and feelings. I'm confident you can do that same thing. Remember, everyone wants to be a winner. Everyone wants to buy in to success. Consider yourself the master who's crafting it for your group.

LOOK AHEAD

❏ Consider visualizing the future of your company two ways. First, hold your own visualization session and document how you see your company maturing. Then, hold a second visualization session with your management team. By comparing the two, you'll see how the two visions differ and what needs to be done to bring them into alignment.

❏ Visualization can also inspire a management group. Are there people in your organization who would benefit from visualizing how their future fits in with the future of the firm?

❏ Do you have a product or service offering that would be a good candidate for visualization? Who should be included in the group?

The Positive Power of Pull

The day my dad and I signed the papers and I acquired ownership of Apollo was a difficult day for me. I was worried now that my dad no longer had skin in the game, he might not choose to stay in the game. I should have known better than to worry; Dad stayed involved. But worrying about him diverted my attention from something else that was going on.

Regime change is never easy. In this small company that my dad ran like an extended family, it was unsettling for much of the staff. That unease was shared with me, and I did my very best to reassure all concerned that there was nothing to be concerned about. The guidance I received at the time from my outside advisers was, "Don't rock the boat. You have a seasoned management team that will support you. Let some time pass and everything will be fine." I should have realized that was conventional thinking.

Before much time had passed, all the members of the management team had made their individual treks to my office to let me know they needed my help to get their jobs done. That was an eye-opener. I expected them to say, "What can we do to help you?"

But instead, I got the reverse. When I questioned them, each said, "Your dad always helped this way."

I pitched in right away and put in a lot of hours helping them. Still, it bothered me. These were well-paid senior people in the organization, and yet they seemed unable to meet the requirements of their jobs. Many of them had been with my dad for years. I talked with him about that and his response was, "They are good people who have been loyal to the company." In other words, because of their length of service, he was giving them a pass on doing their jobs.

I wasn't convinced, however, that these managers—and for that matter the frontline service technicians—couldn't do more. So I began to push them, thinking I could motivate them to take more personal responsibility in fulfilling their jobs. My goal, at that point, was a modest one—I simply wanted them to do the job for which I was paying them. Beyond that, I knew if I wanted the company to grow, I would have to push them even harder. Conventional thinking said the harder I pushed, the better the results should be.

Only it didn't work that way.

I found that when I eased off pushing, they quickly slipped back into lackluster mode. That's one of the frustrations of running a legacy company. Working hard is measured in the number of hours worked, not in the amount accomplished.

I also learned you can only push so many people. It's possible to push five key people in your organization, but the larger the number—ten, twenty, forty, sixty—the harder it becomes. You'd literally need to clone yourself to be in multiple places at the same time.

And finally, you get to a point where you simply can't push any harder. You've done everything within your capacity. There simply isn't any more fuel left in the tank.

I hit that wall. You could have heard the *splat* three states away. It was a low point that had me mentally questioning everything I was doing. *Should I be more like my dad? Was I the right one to be running this company? Was I not doing enough? Was I asking for more than these employees could give? Were we going to go out of business on my watch?* I'd wake up in the middle of the night, night after night, consumed by questions and worries.

My self-examination took me all the way back to that nationals rowing championship in Indianapolis. I found parallels between that race and running the business. I couldn't push that boat to a win. I couldn't move from one rower to another, pushing on his oar, trying to make the boat faster. All I'd have done was create chaos. And that's what my frantic activity was creating now at Apollo. Like rowing, what I had to do was get each manager in the company pulling in sync with a "power 20." I felt that surge of adrenaline that signals an ah-ha moment. I'd shifted into sound thinking mode, and I dubbed this new idea of mine Push Pull Theory.

If I could instill this in the company, my job would be coxswain, calling out the rhythm. The managers would be the rowers, pulling the company forward. It felt right, so right in fact that I tried a test balloon on one of the managers. I phrased it similarly to

JFK's famous "Ask not what your country can do for you, but what you can do for your country."

What I got in return was a lecture on how many years this particular manager had been with the company ("I was here pretty much from the time your dad started up") and that the company owed him for all those years.

In an odd way, his rebuke helped me. For the first time, I realized these guys were working without written systems and processes. To be fair, my dad, who was a process guy, talked about process. However, there was nothing that spelled out in writing the Apollo way of how things were to be handled. Each of my managers was working on the basis of *this is how I (as a manager) see the job.*

If your company operates in this fashion, you have a ticking time bomb on your hands. Sooner or later, probably sooner, you're going to do something one of those managers who possesses your company's knowledge doesn't like. That person will retaliate by withholding the knowledge to show you his or her value. This is a no-win situation for you. You can't let your company be held hostage.

You do have an out, however. By putting systems and processes in place, you can build that institutional knowledge into the mainframe of your business. You'll be replacing personal ways of doing things with the company way.

Again, conventional thinking said start with an employee handbook. I skipped that and started with the process I knew the best—sales. I became a blur of systems and process development. The final piece was an expanded system of scorecards that would allow each person, especially managers, to tally their accomplishments during given time periods.

With the process and system development finished, I rolled it out to the management team. I didn't expect a standing ovation. Institutional change never enjoys rapid assimilation. So I was actually pleased when my efforts received a lukewarm acceptance at least.

The management team now knew what I expected from them, and with our new scorecards it was easy to see who was contributing in a way that pulled the company forward.

During this period, my role shifted from "pusher" to coxswain, calling out instructions to get the team in sync. I wore another hat, too—Coach. I knew these managers were not going to adapt to this new system without help, and I thought coach—not manager, not owner, not CEO—was the best way to do that. I thought some one-on-one coaching might prove to be the difference during the transition. I was trying to move it from one side winning and one side losing to a win/win situation.

But I didn't have any illusions. While I hoped all the managers would embrace this new philosophy, I knew some weren't going to make it. Casualties were going to happen along the way. Either the legacy mentality would be too strong or this was a point in a career where some particular person wasn't about to bend. Whatever the reason, I was prepared that I would receive resignations.

With the new philosophy, systems, and processes in place, I stepped away. I was there to provide direction, there to coach, but I wasn't there to be pulled into doing their jobs. This was the line in the sand. They had to succeed or fail on their own.

Stepping away requires a leap of faith.

Conventional thinking says: "Keep both hands on the wheel. Know where you're going. Don't let the car veer off the road."

You have to get those voices out of your head. Realize that the only way to find out who has the grit to pull the company forward is by letting go and watching what happens.

I was told that was a huge risk. How big of a risk? Let's detail it:

- My greatest concern was that we would alienate our customers. Our work in process would suffer. Future scheduling would become uncertain. Negative customer feedback would create doubts about Apollo's commitment to quality.

- Our most-experienced (senior) techs might decide to go elsewhere. This would cripple our service and installation business. Finding replacements would not be quick, easy, or inexpensive.

- Individual members or the entire management staff might quit. It would be easy for them to say, "This isn't what we signed up for; we're outta here."

- Morale would suffer, making it much more difficult to install new initiatives and move the company forward.

These concerns and more weighed heavily on me. But no matter how great the risks, I had no choice but to take them because a traditional business like Apollo doesn't have the luxury of financial flexibility. It's just simple math.

Based on the number of employees you have and the rates you charge for service, you only have a finite amount of income.

Outgo never stays finite. There are always increases. Manufacturers pass them along. Utilities escalate. Supplies tick up. Gas prices boost transportation costs. And then, there are people needs. A service tech asks for a wage increase of a dollar an hour. This is a guy you'd like to see making more, but you can't bump him up, because the income he's bringing in barely covers his salary, benefits, and overhead.

To be able to afford raises, increases in supplies, and investments in technology to stay current, a traditional business has two choices: raise prices or become more productive.

Actually, there really isn't a choice. All too often, consumers view a traditional business—like heating, cooling, and plumbing—as a commodity. As with any commodity, low price is the name of the game. If you dare to raise prices, your business could literally evaporate.

To survive, to prevail, you have to be more productive, and that means each and every employee has to pull the company forward with increased revenue. The more techs are able to do with their time, the more income they generate for the company, then the more you're able to reward them.

I believed the positive power of Pull was what Apollo needed to help it become the company of choice for employees who wanted to make a difference.

Could the positive power of Pull make your traditional business more productive? I'm convinced that the answer is yes. Most traditional businesses have already trimmed any fat that existed. There aren't more savings to be had. So as you look for ways to offset increases in the cost of doing business, one of the few tools available to you is your staff.

If you move your employees from push mode to Pull mode, you've created an environment in which employees can do more. Properly incentivized, both you and the employees should benefit.

Pull Theory also frees you to do what you should be doing, which is looking forward and see how to best take advantage of the opportunities afforded your company. You can't really do that when your head is down in the weeds.

Think of Pull as a chiropractor. You've got aches and pains in your back that are making everyday tasks harder than they should be. The chiropractor is going to press, pull, prod, and poke. And presto, he or she has your spine back in alignment and suddenly you feel good again.

Pull Theory is about aligning all parts of your organization so that they function at full capacity.

LOOK AHEAD

❏ Do you have your systems and process in writing? If not, make a list of what needs to be formalized, and either tackle this task yourself or put together a team of key individuals to work with you. Make a work plan for accomplishing each project, and set a timetable with key deliverable dates.

❑ Identify who pulls your company forward. These are the people who have embraced the company and made it their own. Reward them. It doesn't have to be with money; it can be verbal recognition. Hold them up as examples of the kinds of employees that make your company stronger. Identify push employees and determine whether a mentoring or coaching arrangement might bring about change.

❑ Develop a plan to replace those who aren't pulling your company forward. While it's hard to imagine replacing people you've know for many years, you're not doing the company justice, and you're actually not helping the employee by allowing him or her to remain in a job that isn't mutually beneficial to both the employee and the company.

❑ Begin to look at the revenue Pull Theory might generate. If you could increase employee productivity by 5 percent, what would that mean to your company? How about 10 percent or even 30 percent? How would this increase in revenue give you a competitive edge in your marketplace? What would it do in terms of the financial needs of your organization?

The Paradox of Leadership

I'd like to tell you that all our managers got with the program and things moved forward swimmingly. I'd like to, but I'd be lying.

Ultimately, we replaced the entire management team. In retrospect, I should have realized that would happen. Also, in retrospect, it was the best thing that could have happened.

The managers who left were good people. But they'd spent too many years working within a legacy model that was no longer sustainable. I call it *The Giving Tree* model after the children's book by Shel Silverstein. It's a wonderful book that I've read to my boys, Jack and Pete, so many times I can almost recite it by heart.

In the book, a boy—over the course of his life—comes to a tree and asks the tree for things the tree can provide—an apple, wood, shade, and so on. The tree always gives of itself happily, and by the time the boy has grown to be an old man, the tree is nothing but a stump. It has no more to give.

Sometimes employees can be like that boy. They ask and ask and ask. But employees have to give back, too; otherwise, the company will become a withered stump of its former self.

We had an older employee who had been with us for a number of years. Because he perceived that he had "seniority" within the company, he expected to be paid more. He was already making more than others, but he constantly wanted an increase. At the same time, because he was "senior" he expected to have his pick of the jobs, and if there was any part of the job he didn't feel like doing, he saw it as his right to delegate that to a junior person. More and more, he wanted to stay at the office and "oversee things." He called it "giving everyone the value of his experience." I called it retiring on the job.

No matter how much I pushed this individual, he wasn't going to move one iota. A traditional business just doesn't have the wherewithal to support his kind of behavior.

Neither can a traditional business enable a greedy owner. Your business is not an ATM for your sole benefit. You can't keep making withdrawal after withdrawal after withdrawal. You have to be the good steward and make deposits.

One of the deposits I made during this crucial transition period was training. I brought in an executive leadership coaching company to work with our management group. It cost big bucks for a company our size. But I thought it was worth it. Outsiders have an independent viewpoint, and I wanted each of these managers to be able to have someone, other than me, to help them learn and grow.

As the executive coaching staff worked their magic, I became more and more aware of how hard it is to develop leadership, and it became evident that our current team had little leadership potential. That's not to say that, individually, they couldn't rise to meet a challenge, but when it came to expanding their sphere of influence to the people who worked for them, the leadership just wasn't there.

In short, they didn't really buy in to Pull Theory, and they couldn't get their people to buy in, either. None of the frontline people—service techs, installers, or salespeople—ever became fully engaged.

When you find a problem like this, don't let it rot. Fix it immediately. When we determined that we were requiring more from these managers than they could provide—even with the systems, processes, and executive leadership training—we knew making the break would be good for them and good for us.

It sounds cruel to say letting someone go is good for that person. But if it isn't a fit, the sooner you acknowledge that and allow them to move on to a position that is a fit, the better it is for both sides.

Let me also add that none of these people were fired by fax. For the sake of discussion, I've lumped their leaving together, but the events happened over a period of several years. And we made sure the partings were as amicable as possible. There were severance packages and letters of recommendation. While I'm not a big believer in rewarding time in grade, these were loyal employees who deserved to be treated with respect.

Each parting was stressful for the organization. We needed to find replacements that could pull the company forward, but we realized no proven performer was going to come to work for us. Why?

It just makes sense when you think about it. People with impressive resumes have made their mark. Those types are looking for challenges we can't provide. A traditional company like ours lacks complexity. It's a relatively simple, repetitive business. It isn't the sort of environment to which an aggressive problem solver naturally gravitates.

Knowing we weren't going to be able to attract proven performers, we set out to find individuals with potential and develop our own talent.

Conventional thinking says just find the right person, put that person in the right seat, and everything will work out. What nobody seems to address is that what feels right might not necessarily be right. Even with candidate assessments and testing, you can still be off.

I looked for three things in this order: motivation, intelligence, and skill. I'm certainly not the first person to hire based on those criteria, but I recognize the sound thinking behind it.

If the person has motivation, he or she is going to seize the opportunity with both hands. If the person has intelligence, he or she is going to use that capacity to make the most of the opportunity. And finally, if he or she doesn't have the skills needed for the job, between the motivation and the intelligence, those skills will quickly be developed.

Here's how it all comes together: We have this motivated, intelligent person who may or may not have the skills needed to fulfill the job on a day-to-day basis. With good systems and processes, we've given that person a solid working foundation. Add good executive coaching and leadership training, and we've given him or her support and confidence. We've created an environment in which he or she can be successful.

So often CEOs hire people, point them in the direction of what they are to do, and then forget about them until the yearly review pops up. That's a mistake. You have to walk a fine line. You need to be there to coach, counsel, and mentor, but also give them enough space so that they don't feel controlled.

This is the big paradox of leadership. This is one of the hardest lessons there is to learn: You actually have more control when you let go.

It's true. Better employees don't want to be controlled. They want to think, not just execute. So if you think you need better managers, you may have to grow your own and give them room to operate.

Think of this as having the greenest grass. How do you get it? Well, you don't covet your neighbor's grass. You have to fertilize your grass and water it regularly. By taking the right steps, you'll grow grass that will have your neighbor coveting your yard. The same is true for employees. Coach, counsel, and mentor. Don't control.

LOOK AHEAD

❏ Do you have a coach, counsel, and mentor program for your employees? Identify those employees who would benefit from one and put a program together. Remember, employees are different. You'll want to tailor your program to fit the particular employee.

❑ Do you have problems you've allowed to linger far too long? Take action and put those problems behind you. If the problems involve an employee, dealing with the problem may be difficult and uncomfortable. But you'll feel better once you've dealt with it and have it behind you.

❑ Do you have a process for employees leaving the company? Consider putting one in place that allows you to part on the best terms possible. Make sure you treat that employee fairly. He or she will speak well or ill of you following their departure. Opt for well.

❑ Are you still hiring based on skills? Or are you also looking for motivation and intelligence? If you shifted your hiring practices to motivation, intelligence, and finally skills, how would that impact your staffing?

6

Capital T, Little t Talent

Oh, yes. I've been fooled in an interview. You probably have, too. So how do you evaluate job candidates, weed out the phonies, and find those rare ones who will prove to be productive employees?

I look at a jam-packed waiting room of candidates, and I see four groups:

- **Capital T's**: Capital T individuals stand out. They have motivation, intelligence, a sense of personal reasonability, and a passion to serve. They are usually very experienced and have a resume that will make you drool.

- **Little t's**: You might cut a Little t some interview slack, thinking the person is shy or even awed to be interviewing with you. Don't go there. The Little t is an individual who blends in. These are the employees who let others do the work, hide under desks, and don't admit to making mistakes.

- **Capital T's in training**: These are diamonds in the rough. They're bright, articulate, and eager to make their mark in business. A Capital T in training inherently understands the power of Pull. Best of all, they welcome all the coaching, counseling, and mentoring you're able to provide.

- **Little t's in Capital T disguise**: These individuals interview extremely well. They're smart, articulate, and likable. They'll tell you how good they are and all the successes they've accomplished. If they come to work for you, don't expect much. It's all talk.

Of course, when it comes to evaluating potential employees, there are all sorts of Myers-Briggs tests you can employ. We use a personality profiling system and find it extremely valuable. But let's first start with my four groups before moving on to personality profiling.

We would all like to hire the Capital T talent. After all, these men and women are the best and the brightest. Not surprisingly, they want to work at larger, leading businesses where they'll receive more opportunity, challenge, and compensation. They view a traditional business as having limited complexity and resources, making it a poor career choice. That's a shame, too. If just a few Capital T's would chose traditional businesses, it could make a huge difference in the dynamic of the traditional business model. Of course, so would unlimited tax breaks.

Little t's in Capital T disguise are a problem. They're foolers. So if you mistakenly hire one, my advice is to remove him or her as quickly as possible. He or she will contaminate your organization. You may not even be aware of the damage being caused, but trust me it's there. Don't wait. Eliminate.

The Capital T's in training are the ones who intrigue me. In the interview, you can usually spot them by their eagerness and inquisitiveness. They vibrate with energy, shooting questions at you a mile a minute. Capital T's in training are often right out of school or may have one job under their belt. On the job, Capital T's in training not only perform, but they're also fun to be around. They make an organization a dynamic workplace. So while they're few and far between, if you have an opportunity to hire one—go for it. You'll be glad you did.

Have the patience to interview enough people. Don't interview three people and take the best of the three because you don't want to spend more of your time with additional candidates. I'd suggest you do short interviews with a broad field of candidates; individually invite those in the top group for longer interviews with a personality profile assessment.

There are a number of personality profile assessment tools available. Most are based on the same four personality quadrants and differ only in the descriptors for the various profiles. Find a system with which you are comfortable and that is easy for you to administer. Using a personality profile gives you an accurate look at the person you're interviewing.

Remember: *For a thirty-minute interview, I can be anybody you want me to be.* The personality profile will tell you the person who will actually show up at work. Personality profiles can tell you things about people like:

- How aggressive or passive they will be.

- How good their social skills are.
- The pace at which they like to work.
- The amount of detail they are capable of handling on the company's behalf.
- How creative they might be.
- The energy level they will bring to the job.

Personality profiles work best if you first do a profile for the position you're looking to fill. Be honest, both in the profile of the position and what you expect from your candidates. We all want to hire superman or superwoman, but what qualities are truly essential to the job?

If you're looking for a salesperson, you definitely want someone with high social skills, and you probably want someone who is comfortable with detail. This would give you a profile of someone who is good at customer service.

If you're hiring someone to run a department, you may want someone who's more aggressive and works at a faster pace. This would give you someone who knows the job to be done and sees that it is accomplished without delay.

Matching the candidate's strengths with those required for the job profile will give you someone who's a good fit for the job. Remember, we all have a finite amount of energy to utilize at work. The more productive employee is the one who is using that energy to do a job that is compatible with his or her talents and interests. People who are trying to do a job that isn't really compatible with their personality have to use much more energy. So don't expect a shy, introverted person to be successful as a gregarious salesperson. Don't expect the gregarious people person to be happy stuck in a back office alone. Structure compatibility. It breeds happiness. And happiness in the workplace is often contagious.

Personality profiles also help you build a management team that works together without conflict. As team members learn each other's strengths, drives, and needs, they develop an understanding of how best to interact using their unique personalities. That understanding helps build rapport and avoids turf battles and disagreements.

If you don't want to do the work of developing a Capital T in training, there is one place—and it's often overlooked—where you might discover a Capital T.

There are many Capital T women who have left the workforce to raise a family and, now that their children have started school, are looking for part-time work—usually twenty or thirty hours a week.

Many of these women have their PhD or MBA. They've often received expensive training from their former employers. They offer a traditional business a rare chance to bring on board the talent and insight usually monopolized by the big guys.

With our rapid growth, Apollo had the need for a Human Resources director. This was not a position where I thought we could afford to hire a Capital T in training and mentor that person over time. We needed someone with knowledge who could hit the ground running.

We were fortunate to find a woman who had been the HR director for a Fortune 500 company before leaving to start her family. We structured a working agreement for twenty hours a week, some of which could be done from home. Her comment during the interview sold me. "I'll get more done in twenty hours," she said, "than most people will in forty." She's done it, too. She's a whirlwind and happy to be back in the workplace in an arrangement that allows her to balance work and family without stress.

The most important job that a CEO handles could be hiring. Think of yourself as a football coach. What if you had a second-rate offensive line? You'd have problems no matter what offensive scheme you were trying to run. Look at your organization in this way and bolster talent where you need to.

Don't settle. Find the person you consider best for the job.

LOOK AHEAD

❏ Take a look at your org chart. Next to each position, pencil in whether you consider this person a Capital T, Little t, Capital T in training, or Little t in Capital T disguise. Think about the changes that might make you a stronger organization. Are there spots where you could coach, counsel, and mentor a Capital T in training? Are there spots where a part-time Capital T could add value by offering big-company talent and insight?

❏ What are your hiring needs? Are you frustrated trying to attract Capital T talent? Would a Capital T in training make sense for your organization? Put together a coach, counsel, and mentoring program that would allow you to grow your own Capital T's in training.

❏ Does a personality profiling assessment make sense in your business? Could it make your management team more cohesive? Could it help you spot Capital T's in training?

❏ Are you in a position to take advantage of one of the largest available talent pools—women who are looking to rejoin the workforce after starting a family? What positions in your company would benefit from the talent and knowledge of a part-time Capital T?

Squirrel Versus Dog

If you want to climb a tree, hire a squirrel. He'll scamper right up that tree, as fast as his little feet will take him. If you want to climb a tree, don't hire a dog. Oh, a dog will be your friend. He'll sit at the bottom, look up the tree, and bark. But climb? Seriously?

Yet all the time dogs get hired to do squirrel work. Why is that? It's actually by default. You see, if you hire a Capital T or Capital T-in-training squirrel, he or she is going to move very fast in climbing that tree. These talented people are in a rush to make things happen. They associate work with quality, not quantity. And by quality of work, I'm talking about the depth of that intellectual challenge. They want to know: "Is this a stimulating work situation?"

The answer for most traditional businesses is that this is not a stimulating situation. The work here, for the most part, is repetitive and routine. That makes for bored squirrels. Dogs, however, seem to settle right in. They find the situation comforting. The objective of climbing the tree may never be reached, but as they sit around the bottom of the tree, their tails will definitely be wagging.

Because there are so few squirrels in traditional business, those businesses are seldom nimble or quick to adapt. Heck, in most traditional businesses, each year passes like the year before it. Dogs like routine. They want to know dinner will be served in the blue bowl and will magically appear at the northeast corner of the kitchen at exactly five o'clock each evening. If something should happen to change the routine—even if it's a customer request or something that would benefit the customer—they cover their face with their paws. This is one of the core problems of attempting to innovate in a traditional business. Try it and listen to the dogs howl.

If you'll allow me, I'd like to make one more animal analogy, this one about horses:

I would rather have an organization of thirty thoroughbreds than sixty quarter horses. Why is that?

Thoroughbreds do one thing—run. They like to go as hard and as fast as they can.

Quarter horses are working horses. You see them at rodeos, horse shows, and working ranches. They're well suited to herding cattle or calf roping.

My point is that thoroughbreds are the better breed for pulling an organization forward. The have the speed and the spirit that propels an organization along. And they have determination. They run to the point of exhaustion.

Quarter horses do the work, but they watch the time clock. They don't pull. They know all that reining, roping, and herding will be there tomorrow. They simply don't have the will to positively impact an organization.

At Apollo, we hire every thoroughbred we can. But like squirrels, they're hard to find. And again, I think that puts a limit on how large you can grow a traditional business at any one location. There simply aren't enough thoroughbreds available to help a traditional business grow beyond fifty or sixty people.

So if you have intentions of growing larger, how do you attract more squirrels and thoroughbreds?

I'm convinced you have to become the company of choice. You need to make your business the place where everyone wants to work. Right now, who doesn't want to work at Google, Facebook, or Apple? These have become the employers of choice. A generation ago it was GM, Ford, and GE. These are all big companies that had the resources and challenges to attract the best and the brightest.

But smaller, traditional companies can become an employer of choice, too. Take pizza parlors. Every town has multiple pizza companies. But talk to the kids who work at these places—the servers, delivery people, even the kids who toss the pies—and they'll tell you there's one place that's heads and shoulders better than all the others. It's the place they all want to work. It's the company of choice.

What's the difference? How did one place get to be so special? I believe it starts at the top. Founder. Owner. CEO. President. The title doesn't matter. This person understood leadership and did the right things right. Not some of the right things. Not the right things almost right. To be the company of choice, you have to do all the right things right.

Don't panic. It's doable.

I would like to be able to tell you that the most important factor is a nurturing environment, because I believe finding someone who will coach, counsel, and mentor you early in your career can change the trajectory of your growth and achievement. However, we live in the real world, so let's not tiptoe around the truth—which is that the most important factor in becoming a company of choice is money. Surprise, surprise.

While most people would probably pay the company or at least work for practically nothing to be at Apple or Facebook, the same is not true at a traditional company. Traditional companies can't offer life on the cutting edge. There's no mission to change the way we communicate or to advance better living. Because we can't offer something altruistic, compensation becomes a bigger attraction. And I'm not talking big money here. In many cases, what we're talking about is hourly—if you pay a dollar or two more an hour, it can take you much closer to being the employer of choice.

Paying that slightly higher wage might be the smartest thing you could do. It will allow you to attract better employees, and it will improve retention. Companies that have 100 percent or more in turnover every year are bleeding money. The costs to recruit and train that many new people often go unrecognized, but they are significant.

After compensation comes the nurturing environment. If a person is being paid adequately and has the training and support he or she needs to feel good about the job, usually that person is a happy employee. Kick it up a notch, and imagine how employees feel if their managers have a plan or a program that will help them advance in the organization. That single step changes a job into a career. Few companies have advancement paths in place, but once the word gets out that you have a program like that, employees will seek you out.

The third big thing to me is image. Nobody wants to work in some disgusting hole. I remember visiting manufacturing companies on behalf of Entrepreneurs' Organization (EO), an organization in which I'm active. The first company's lobby was small, dark, and one wall was covered in orange shag carpet left over from the seventies. On the wall were a series of photos that were so sun damaged they appeared to be framed pieces of white paper. There were two chairs in the lobby—one had a hole in the seat, the other was missing an arm.

The management team I met seemed just like the lobby. Old. Tired. Bored. Company of choice? Not on your life.

Same trip. Different manufacturing company. This company's building wasn't any newer, nor was the lobby any bigger. But framed on the walls were blowups of the company's latest advertising series. I was reminded that this company had great buzz in the marketplace. That marketing campaign gave you the impression they were taking their industry by storm. The management team I met with was older but not stodgy. They saw themselves as vital and the company as vibrant. Through a little research I learned that the marketing campaign had jump-started the company. They'd found their voice, their buzz, and eventually their status as an employer of choice.

Still on that trip. Yet another manufacturing company. This one was in a brand-new building with well-furnished executive offices in front, an entire wing of labs for R&D, and a spacious two-story plant floor complete with product demonstration space. They gave a great tour. The place was visually exciting. The CEO told me they brought in Capital T-in-training students from the best schools in their field and wowed them with the tour. It wowed me. I wanted to work there. It definitely was an employer of choice.

Success breeds success. Do one thing that enhances your attractiveness—compensation, facilities, buzz, nurturing—and doing the next one is easier. Likewise, when you add better people, you become more attractive to the next group of thoroughbreds and squirrels.

LOOK AHEAD

❑ It may sound silly, but list key employees and classify them as either a squirrel or a dog. Do their roles fit them? Or would you be better off finding a different person for that job?

❑ How are the thoroughbreds in your organization pulling the company forward? How can you monetize this positive behavior?

❑ Who do you think is your competition? What would it take for you to become the employer of choice?

Making the Circles
Concentric

Recruiting good talent is one thing. Retaining it is quite another. I had a fellow CEO who confided in me that he didn't have trouble recruiting, but he couldn't keep anybody for long. "They just turn in their notice," he said, shaking his head. The man ran a mid-sized manufacturing business, made a quality product, and had been in business for over fifteen years. On the surface, he ran a good shop.

As I questioned him, however, fault lines began to appear. I asked him if he had job descriptions for his positions. "No." I asked if he had clear reporting channels. "No." I asked if he had management team meetings. "No." Before I could ask the next question, he said, "I have no need of that stuff. If anyone needs anything, all they have to do is ask me."

Alarm bells started going off in my head.

I asked one more question to be sure: "Do your managers have their own budgets?" He said, *"No. If they need money, they see me about it."*

Ouch. Here's what was happening. Every person in the

company—about sixty in all—from the EVP to the receptionist reported to this CEO. No department had a budget. If a department head needed money to buy anything—printer paper or a numerically controlled machine—they had to go to the CEO for an authorization. He would decide whether to spend the money or not.

It was sort of like going to your dad, saying you needed $20 for a date, and having him look in his wallet, shuffle through the bills, and say, "Sorry, not today."

Talk about demoralizing. But this was just the tip of the iceberg.

Each department head was held fully responsible. For example, the VP of Manufacturing was responsible for the production of this much product on this timetable at this cost. If the VP of Manufacturing didn't meet her production schedules, she was verbally reprimanded, and there were salary ramifications. What the VP of Manufacturing didn't have was authority commensurate with the responsibility. She couldn't, for example, order more raw materials without going to the CEO for approval. She couldn't authorize overtime hours without going to the CEO for approval.

And when she did go to the CEO, what happened? Well, "Dad" would grudgingly dig out his wallet, look inside, and depending on what he saw or what his mood happened to be that day, say yeah or nay.

Demoralized, the poor VP of Manufacturing would shuffle back to her office and try to figure out a Plan B. Would you want to stay long in that job? Me neither.

And imagine, she had to line up at the door to see Dad. The receptionist might be ahead of her, asking for money to buy stamps.

The VP of Sales might be behind the receptionist to ask if the CEO could okay a sales contract.

The VP of Human Resources might be behind him to ask if the CEO would okay a maternity leave.

Again, would you stay in that nuthouse? No talented person would stay longer than it took for him or her to find the next job.

So what's the moral here? There are several. In my opinion, being a CEO is not about getting to make all the decisions. It may flatter your ego, but ultimately it's self-defeating. What if that CEO goes on vacation? What if he's sick? Does the place come to a grinding halt? In this case, the answer was yes.

A good CEO should be thinking of the company first. If he gets hit by a bus tomorrow, there should be someone in line to carry on. The company shouldn't miss a beat.

But the bigger lesson to be learned here is one of responsibility and authority.

Imagine two circles on a piece of paper in front of you. The circle on the left is labeled Responsibility; the one on the right is Authority.

In the case of this manufacturing company, the two circles are kept far apart. Now imagine the two circles overlapping the way they do in the MasterCard logo. Picture that little overlapping space shaded in. The employee now has Authority for this much of his or her Responsibility. As the overlapping shaded area becomes greater, the employee has more authority for the job for which he or she is responsible.

Now imagine Authority directly on top of Responsibility. The two circles appear to be in perfect alignment. This is what a talented person is looking for: complete authority for his or her area of responsibility.

Why is this so crucial? It allows that person to exercise his or her good judgment in a way that is positive for the individual—assuming you have the right person in the position—and for the company.

Detailing this authority commensurate with responsibility early in the hiring practice may make you more attractive to Capital T's or Capital T's-in-training talent. It will certainly help you retain good talent because it builds responsibility and emotional investment in the firm.

At Apollo, my management team has alignment in authority and responsibility, but we've taken it a step further and divided the company into business units. Each manager has complete responsibility and authority for his or her business unit. In effect, each manager is running his or her own company.

This is the ultimate way to attract good talent.

LOOK AHEAD

❏ How are responsibility and authority divided in your organization? Who has responsibility but little authority? Who has a great deal of authority but little responsibility? Is there a more equitable arrangement that would be more productive for the company?

❏ How would a better alignment of responsibility and authority make your organization more effective? Would it empower employees to be more productive? Would it eliminate confusion and allow the organization to run smoother?

❏ Is responsibility and authority clear within your management team? This is one of the areas where having a gray area can cause power struggles and discord. Making lines of authority clear eliminates the potential for trouble.

❏ Be honest. Are there key areas of authority you have withheld from your team? Why? Remember the paradox of leadership. You have more control by letting go.

9

Is Implosion Imminent?

You'd think—because we've hired good people and given them authority commensurate with responsibility—day-to-day operations within the company would run as smooth as a high-priced silk necktie.

Ha. The fun is just beginning.

Squirrels and thoroughbreds almost always don't play well with others. The qualities that we like about them—that they're goal-oriented, assertive, independent, competitive, and venturesome—mean they're going to fight among themselves.

Even if you've segmented their responsibilities by product line or by function, traditional companies are just too small not to have overlap. What do I mean by overlap? No part of a company truly operates on its own. For example, when a customer buys a new furnace, the sale is complete. But the salesman is the first to hear the customer's complaint if the install goes badly. Now it would be great if the head of sales and the head of installation worked seamlessly for the good of the company. And once in a blue moon (whatever that is) it happens. Most times, however, what these two people do is butt heads. Check out this example:

Install claims that Sales didn't quote the job right.

Sales counters that Install doesn't know what they're doing.

Install stops the job to make a point.

The customer calls to complain; Sales says not my fault.

They can't help themselves. A strong-minded problem solver never sees the other person doing the job as well as he or she could. And he or she isn't shy about letting people know it. If a problem crops up on the job, he or she will definitely be pointing a finger and adamantly saying how things should have been handled— even if that discussion is to the detriment of the company.

You have to realize, these achievers aren't doing this maliciously. They genuinely believe they could do a better job. Every thoroughbred believes he has the bloodline to win the race. Each squirrel believes he can run the fastest. But what starts as a petty squabble can build into turf wars or, worse, power plays.

Many traditional companies have come to a complete stop as two or three thoroughbreds fought to the death.

I heard a story about a company where a rift developed between the heads of two product lines. Both were vying for manufacturing time in the plant. One befriended the plant manager; the other tried to bully the plant manager by accusing him of not getting his work done. The situation became so bitter and unproductive that the owner had to replace both product heads. Because each man held the institutional knowledge about his line, this was a huge setback for the organization. Although the plant manager was retained, he was distrustful of the replacement product heads. Ultimately, he retired early. All this over what? Ego. Each man was trying to eclipse the other.

So what do you do? After all, you need these highly competitive people to pull the company forward.

First, let's recognize what we're dealing with here. It is most definitely a need for control. These individuals thrive on proving themselves, mastering the big picture, acting independently, and solving problems. They don't want to be managed, don't feel the need for reassurance, nor need the security of a drama-free workplace. To these individuals, nothing matters but achievement.

Understanding this person's dominant drive points to ways to channel this competitive desire.

SET CHALLENGES

Give these people something on which to bring their considerable talents to bear. Remember, these people are problem solvers. So if you give them a customer-focused problem to solve, they will knock down walls to complete that task. Consider what will happen if you don't supply them with a problem: They will find something internally to break so that they will have something to fix. Keep raising the bar with your challenges. Stay a step ahead, and you'll be amazed at what thoroughbreds and squirrels are able to accomplish for your company.

INCENTIVIZE PROPER BEHAVIOR

While these competitive individuals are all about control and achievement, they respond well to compensation plans that reward that behavior. The trick is to design your compensation plan for them in such a way that it causes them to stay focused on customer problems and not create internal strife. Recognition in the way of awards or perks also has a positive effect. These individuals seek out recognition for their ideas, and when you publicly compliment them, it pays huge dividends in the form of proper behavior.

ENCOURAGE CAMARADERIE

It's harder to fight a friend. So before things get combative, if you can get employees to become friends, it may head off trouble. Invite them and their spouses over for a Saturday Bar-B-Que. See a ball game together. Have your key people go together to an out-of-town seminar. All of these things have little cost but will give your people shared experiences and a common purpose.

PROVIDE IMMEDIATE FEEDBACK

If you hear about or see behavior that will lead to internal strife, take that person aside and immediately let them know such behavior is not acceptable. If you don't, that inappropriate behavior may become a competition. That's why you want to step in before it starts to escalate. If they continue the unacceptable behavior, put them on a work plan. Although you'll keep the work plan private, word will spread, sending a signal throughout the organization.

ESTABLISH A CHAIN OF COMMAND

And finally, have a chain of command for when you're out of the office. Leaving a vacuum at the top—even for a short period of time—is like putting blood in the water for sharks. Your squirrels or thoroughbreds won't be able to help themselves. Each will try and muscle up and be "you" while you're gone.

There's a true story about General Alexander Haig, President Nixon's chief of staff at the time of Nixon's resignation. As the helicopter carrying the first family left the White House lawn, Haig was telling anyone who'd listen, "I'm in charge. I'm in charge." Haig was a good soldier, made to look comical trying to be the first to fill that important empty chair. Don't put any of your people in that situation.

When you're out of the office for a period of time, designate one of your key people to be in charge. Try rotating the responsibility and authority among your key lieutenants. It will show that you don't favor one more than another, and it will give you a chance to see how each performs in your absence.

I was at a lunch with two fellow business owners. One was complaining that his three department heads were always at each other's throats. "You're lucky," the other owner told him. "My top people don't do anything unless I yell at them."

Managing squirrels and thoroughbreds can be a challenge. But, you know, it's actually a happy problem to have.

LOOK AHEAD

❏ For each of your key squirrels/thoroughbreds, put together a road map of challenges you'd like them to solve. If possible, tie monetary compensation to the achievement of set challenge levels.

❏ Plan a camaraderie event to build shared experiences with key team members. Seminars are often ways to build camaraderie and provide an outside perspective that helps develop meaningful discussion within your group.

❏ Use personality profiling to put key people in the right order. Don't have a person who's good at detail supervising a big-picture person. Don't have a low social skills person as the head of your sales force. Put together an org chart with each person's name, and underneath it put that person's profile, dominant drive, and talents. Are the profiles in alignment? Are the drives in conflict? Are there moves that would put the right drives in the right places? Remember, having a social butterfly stocking the warehouse is an accident waiting to happen.

10

All in the Family

Growing up, I never had illusions that I lived on Easy Street because my dad owned Apollo. At the time, it was the last place I wanted to work. My plan was to take the rowing world by storm and, after a momentous career, become a rowing coach. I never had that sense of entitlement that so many children of business owners have. I never thought I was owed a big paycheck no matter how little I did just because my name happened to be Gerdsen. Nor, after I joined the company, did my dad give me special treatment because I was his son.

As I look around, I see that we were an atypical family business. Usually family trumps good business practices, and that can doom the business to griping and sniping. Let me give you a couple of examples.

One traditional business with which I'm familiar has two sons— each listed as a vice president of the company—who rarely come into the office. On those days when they don't put in an appearance, the staff is left to make excuses for their absence and put off needed decisions. When they do come in, they like to order people around to flex their authority muscles. As you might imagine, resentment is always about to boil over. The few staffers brave enough to go to Dad and voice a well-intended word of concern—get the proverbial boot.

What was a good business is now a toxic environment. No wonder the company keeps declining. You only have to look at the second generation's work ethic to know the end is near.

In another traditional business, Mom runs the business with an iron hand. Her son, he of the exalted title and exorbitant salary, has no authority but does have responsibility for all the business's operations. He and Mom are constantly fighting. If she says, "Buy," then he says, "Sell." If he says, "Green," then she insists on blue. Staffers talk about daylong meetings where the two yell at each other. Work there? Just shoot me and put me out of my misery.

In another traditional business, Dad has put his children in all the key positions. The problem is they are just collecting paychecks while they pursue other interests. Those kids are the epitome of mid-level managers—their job is to keep important things from happening.

I mention these examples because family businesses usually get a good rap. That happens when outsiders envision some sort of Norman Rockwellesque workplace. But how do the nonfamily people who work there feel?

If you're a nonfamily employee in a family business, you have to understand the double standard that's in play. Family members are held to a very different set of rules, well, basically no rules. No double standard is ever good, but in the case of a family-run traditional business, it's demoralizing and demotivating.

What squirrel or thoroughbred wants to work in an organization where he or she is treated as a second-class citizen? A thoroughbred at a family business took the owner a well-thought-out business plan for adding a complementary product line. Dad looked it over, nodded, and even said, "Good work." Then he gave it to his son, who put his fingerprints all over it prior to implementation. When the new product line failed to perform, the son blamed the employee for the line's poor performance, and the employee was let go. Fair? Of course not. But in this kind of environment, you know if something goes wrong it's never going to be the fault of a family member.

Even Capital T's in training quickly size up the situation and realize they'd be better off elsewhere. Because it is often impossible to get good ideas through the family filter, few business-building initiatives ever reach the marketplace.

I liken this situation to treading water with weights tied to your body. It's not a matter of will; it's a matter of when the firm goes under.

These businesses, obviously, will never make the transition from Push to Pull. It's hard to get employees to pull when the fruits of their labors are being attributed to family members. Ironically, just to do their jobs properly, employees may have to push family members out of the way.

Am I being too hard on family-run traditional businesses? Probably. But I offer this criticism in the spirit of gun safety. It's easy to shoot yourself in the foot. Know the damage you can cause before all your toes are gone.

My sons, Pete and Jack, are a long way from entering the workaday world, and they may not want anything to do with Apollo. But just as my dad hoped I wanted to work with him, I hope they will want to work with me.

If they do, there will be some ground rules:

- You get no special treatment because your last name happens to be Gerdsen.
- You work in all areas of the business, learning it from the ground up.
- You advance as you're able to pull the company forward.
- You make the average salary of others at that same position.
- Because your name is Gerdsen, you're expected to do more business, tackle the toughest problems, spend the late nights, and show (not tell) how to pull the business forward.

Yeah, it's tough love. But in a family business, there can't be any other kind.

LOOK AHEAD

❏ If you're a family-run traditional business, do you have one standard for your children and another for employees? How could you level the playing field? How would that be good for your employees? How would that be good for your children?

❏ If you have multiple children in the business, is being fair to all holding back one that could pull the business forward? How can you manage to get the best from each of your children?

Mindset and Motivation

Are you a squirrel? Are you a thoroughbred? Or are you a dog? Don't be offended. I'm asking for a reason.

MINDSET

Success is a mindset. If you—as the leader of the organization—don't believe the company will be successful, wow, the company is going to struggle. So it's important, resorting here to a cliché, that you *get your head in the game.*

That means if you don't automatically relate to being a squirrel or thoroughbred—if you hesitated for even a second—we need to get rid of your head trash.

Head trash?

Yep, we've all got it. Here's mine:

I've got a learning disability.

I'm not as smart as the other kids.

I'll never have good enough grades to go to college.

I'm not good enough to compete with the best.

Who would want to buy from me?

What do I know about running a business?

If I lose my management team, I'm finished.

Where am I ever going to find good talent?

If I add another product line will it be a fiasco?

I could go on, but you get the idea. It's the negative thoughts and comments that we've had or heard since we've been little kids. I call it head trash.

And the insidious thing about head trash is that it can defeat you before you even get started and, guess what, you don't even recognize it's happening.

As a business leader you have to cleanse head trash from your mind. You can't let it interfere with your decision-making ability.

I knew the head of an electrical contracting company. Sharp guy. Smart. Outgoing. Personable. Good to his people. But when it came to making business decisions, you could almost see him withdraw into himself. More than that, he'd go out of his way to avoid having to make a decision. I always wondered why he was so reticent. Finally, I learned what it was. We were at a ball game, chatting about this and that, and he just blurted it out.

He'd never gone to college. His head trash was that he'd been told he wasn't smart enough. Because of that, he lived in fear that—being dumb—he'd make the wrong decision.

I sympathized. His head trash, like mine, had been there a long time. Getting rid of head trash that's almost as old as you are isn't easy.

What worked for me may work for you. Find a group of positive people and join it. I joined Entrepreneurs' Organization (EO) because I wanted the learning opportunities they offered. It was perfect for that. I went through EO Leadership Academy and the EO Entrepreneurial Masters Program. I learned a ton. But the real benefit was that it put me shoulder to shoulder with my business peers. In talking with them, I discovered we were pretty much on par. Years of head trash melted away.

The more I worked within EO, the more I realized these guys were actually interested in my ideas and what I had to say. Talk about a revelation. Suddenly, I wasn't the big, dumb kid anymore. The confidence I gained from EO was immeasurable. And I'm confident you'll have the same experience if you let your group of positive people help you take the trash out.

Once you get rid of that head trash, stay positive. Make a conscious effort to avoid all negative thought.

I'm not sure if I can do that. Boot it.

This might be too much for me to handle. It's outta here.

Other people are better at this. Kick it to the curb.

Eliminating all negative thought is tough. It takes real discipline. But the reward is well worth it. Your entire organization will reap the benefits.

Now that we've dealt with your mindset, we need to work on your motivation. The two really do go hand in hand.

MOTIVATION

Motivation is that desire to make things happen. And again, if you don't have the desire to run your organization and pull it forward to success, then you've doomed your employees to living in a pretty uninspiring place.

Mediocrity doesn't get anyone's juices flowing.

For me, motivation was finding out just how much I could do, how far I could go. I've always had that drive to push the limits. (And conversely that fear that I haven't done enough.)

In my early sales days at Apollo, I had a customer who gave me a different look at motivation. The man was just starting out in his business career. On a sales visit to his office, he showed me a folder he kept in his top drawer. In that folder were pages he'd torn from magazines. He called it his "reminder" folder. Here's what his folder contained:

A photo of a beach house with a million-dollar view of the water. *This is the house I want to own.*

A photo of a 40-foot yawl under full sail. *This is the boat I want to own.*

A photo of a Porsche 911. *This is the car I want to own.*

An article about a prestigious local country club. *This is the club I want to join.*

A photo feature on fly-fishing in Montana. *This is the vacation I want to take.*

And there was more. Right down to the gold Rolex he wanted. Every morning, before he started work, he told me he looked through that folder and it got him pumped up for the day.

That's what worked for him.

Motivation for you may be monetary. *I want to make a million dollars.* It may be recognition. *I want to be the best-known firm in town.* It may be stature. *I want an executive position within our organization.* Or it may be emotional. *I want the respect and admiration of the staff.*

Use what works for you; let that motivation pull you forward. The great thing about motivation is that it's viral. If you're motivated, others in the organization will be motivated as well.

Put a positive mindset together with motivation, and you've become a force to be reckoned with. This is the person who can lead a company forward. The new you. One of my favorite quotes sums it up nicely:

The future isn't in front of you. It's inside you.

SQUIRRELS, BOATS, AND THOROUGHBREDS

LOOK AHEAD

❑ Surround yourself with positive people. Find a group and join it. More than that, get involved. Your involvement will help you get to know people at a deeper level and make the experience more meaningful.

❑ Examine your head trash. Make a list of it and remember how it came to be. More important, next to each thing, list all the times it hasn't been true.

❑ Goals are wonderful things. Begin to explore ways motivation might drive you and your business.

The Communications Conundrum

We have all these ways of communicating, but nobody talks the truth.

Smart phones. Texting. Twittering. Facebook. My dad just shakes his head. I have to agree with him. We have all these ways of staying connected to each other, but the art of honest communication seems to be disappearing.

To me, this is a huge problem. Because once you align your management team, you need to align your communications structure. I don't mean put the company news on your Facebook page. I mean set the standard that your company expects face-to-face honest dialog when important communications need to be made.

There are two keys here: face-to-face and honest.

FACE-TO-FACE COMMUNICATION

That first one is especially important to me. Remember, I'm the guy whose boss was fired by fax. And lest you think that doesn't happen anymore, think again. It does, only with newer technology.

One of my service techs got a text message that his girlfriend was breaking up with him. Is that gutless or what?

When it comes to communication, no employee wants to hear bad news. No employer wants to deliver bad news. But to be fair to that employee, you need to have that discussion in a way that turns a deficit meeting into a positive outcome.

By meeting face-to-face, you communicate so much more than just words. Making time for that employee shows that you value that person. He or she has the benefit of the sincerity with which you convey your message. And he or she has the opportunity to ask questions so that you can address any misconceptions or concerns.

I had a friend who owned a traditional business, and during a slowdown he was forced to let five people go. He chose to meet with them as a group, probably thinking it would be easier and less time consuming for him. After he broke the news, he realized the awkward situation he'd created. He spent more time trying to make amends than he would have if he'd met with each person individually.

Make the time. Then make the session meaningful. This is a crucial moment in an employee's career, and by your actions, you can make it a positive experience.

HONEST COMMUNICATION

Be truthful. You may think you are making things better by couching things in platitudes, but you're not. Forget political correctness for once. We all want to be told the truth. We're all suspicious when we're told less than the truth.

So why is it that so little truth gets communicated? Part of it is a fear of being politically incorrect. Fear that someone is going to point a finger at you and say that you're prejudiced. Fear that this innuendo is somehow going to hurt your reputation. And then, there's the fact that we don't want to hurt anyone. We don't want to be responsible for upsetting anybody by pointing out negative qualities.

Instead of telling job applicants, "You didn't get the job because you engage in a certain specific type of unacceptable behavior, which might have some negative consequences and cause you to miss significant periods of work," we say, "Sorry, we don't think you're qualified for the position."

These applicants are left scratching their heads as to why they weren't hired. We also haven't given them the feedback they need to get the next job. This was all in the name of political correctness. Wouldn't the truth have been better?

In any high-performance organization, the leader must have the ability to deliver the truth in a way that it is viewed as a favorable learning experience. Only by telling the truth—by being authentic—will you create trust and strong relationships.

People with different management styles handle authenticity in different ways. I imagine Steve Jobs had a different communication style from Warren Buffett. Oprah Winfrey's style is probably quite different from that of Larry Page and Sergey Brin, who founded Google. And they're all different from my dad, who founded

Apollo. But each, in his or her own unique style, has found a way to deliver the truth as a favorable learning experience.

That's especially difficult in a large multicultural corporation. Because in that situation you have to deliver your message in the most broad and deep way that comes across as favorable to all parties. Now when I say favorable, I mean favorable in the outcome of the message to be truthful and understood, not the outcome to be "Wow, I didn't make it, but I feel pretty good about it."

Being honest with people increases your credibility. People realize you don't have hidden agendas and that you say what you mean.

How has that worked here at Apollo? Because I'm pretty loud and outspoken, it's helped considerably. People know not to be intimidated by the volume but to listen to the message. My managers know they're free to say what they think, not what I want to hear. They also know if there's something important—good or bad—it needs to be communicated.

They say bad news travels fast. I don't think it travels at all. You have to go searching for it. Gather a group around the table and watch how the faces go blank at the mention of bad news. No one wants any of the damage to spill over onto him or her. Yet, getting bad news out in the open so it can be dealt with quickly is crucial.

There's that old saw: "Fix the problem, not the blame." I couldn't agree more, and I think honest face-to-face communication can make that happen. At Apollo, I welcome bad news because then I know it's not out there unspoken waiting to develop into a train wreck.

When there is a problem and something is done incorrectly, I get the group together for a teachable moment. In the past, I would have taken the opportunity to scream and holler. Now, I look at the opportunity differently. It's something I learned from my son Jack when he was five. He'd done something he knew wasn't right and thought I was going to punish him. Instead, we had a conversation about it. We talked about the difference between right and wrong, discussed what he could do to make it right, and what he could do to prevent it from happening again. He learned from that talk. So did I.

Of course there are plenty of these stories in business. The most famous is about Thomas Watson Sr., the founder of IBM. One of his salesmen made a mistake that cost IBM a $20 million order. The salesman was summoned to Watson's office and was sure he was about to be fired. Watson looked the man over and asked him what he'd learned from his mistake.

"What I've learned?" the man asked, somewhat taken aback. "I was expecting to be fired."

"Nonsense," Watson told him. "I've just spent $20 million educating you."

Or as Rahm Emanuel, President Obama's former chief of staff, famously said, "You never want a serious crisis to go to waste."

Use the opportunities you're given to move your organization forward with truthful communication and teachable moments. You might be surprised at the positive effect it will have on your entire organization.

LOOK AHEAD

❏ How do you view communication in your company? How do you think your employees view it?

❏ Are there teachable moments you could use to help your management team? Are you able to extend that to your frontline people?

❏ Is your communication style keeping with the way you want your company to operate? If not, how might you change it to bring it more into alignment?

Three to Go

At Apollo, change is constant. We have three initiatives going at any one time. Strategic planners always want you to do a top five. But I've found five initiatives are too many for an organization. Three seems to create a sense of energy in the organization, a feeling that the company is moving forward and becoming better. More than three—chaos erupts. Too much is in flux.

Initiatives are programs of improvement. We select a process or system that can be improved and design a work plan to accomplish that improvement.

My dad used to pay everyone on legacy—length of service to the company. Nowhere was contribution to the company in that equation. We had some service techs, new to the company, who were making a big contribution but earning very little. We had some managers who were making a lot but had retired on the job.

It wasn't fair. And it wasn't good for the company.

We've just completed our biggest initiative to date. Working with outside advisers, we crafted a performance-based compensation plan. Employees get a base pay and then earn a percentage based on drivers such as customer satisfaction indexes, gross margin, and top-line revenue.

In this system if you're a service tech and you handle ten customer service calls, you would receive the service tech base pay plus a percentage of the income generated by those ten service calls.

If you're a more motivated service tech and, during the same period of time, you handle fifteen service calls, you're going to earn more money based on your percentage for those additional five calls.

And lest you think guys will start speeding through their service calls, there are quality checks and customer satisfaction numbers that must be met as well.

Here's the way I look at it. If you're asking your employees to pull you along, it's important to reward them for their efforts. And there's no fairer way to do that than to pay for performance.

To our service techs, being able to make more money has been huge. They're psyched because they're bringing home a bigger paycheck, and that always feels good. Their spouses feel good because they know the bills are going to get paid and there might even be enough money to take the kids on a nice vacation. It's not just the techs who benefit from this new initiative; it's that person's whole family.

Someone reading this, possibly you, has a hand up, asking, "Why did you go to this complicated base plus percentage system; why didn't you just do bonuses?"

Fair question. I heard a great urban myth about the pitfalls of bonuses. Whether the story is true or not, the lesson sure is.

It seems there was a large company, which shall remain

nameless, in Hershey, Pennsylvania. This company experienced a very good year. An excellent year, in fact. So good a year that management wanted to do something special to say thank you to all the employees. After some deliberation, they decided to give each employee a holiday turkey.

In secret, a team bought up virtually every turkey in the Hershey area and, one day early in December, each employee was presented with the company's thanks and a turkey as a token of gratitude.

This came as a complete surprise to the employees and was greeted by a huge outpouring of good feeling for the company. Management basked in the glow. It was a love fest of epic proportions. Until . . .

In the fall of the following year, management heard that employees were whispering among themselves, "Wonder if we're going to get turkeys this year?"

Well, that year, the company wasn't having an especially good year and wasn't thinking about turkeys at all. In the company's mind, the turkeys had been a one-time bonus.

As the whispering continued, the company management began to reconsider. After all, they didn't want to be seen as Scrooges and, the year before, the employees had been really thankful and appreciative. So they decided, even though the year hadn't been that good, turkeys again for everyone.

Early in December, on the same day as the previous year, each employee was given a turkey. Only this time, the reaction was a little different. Instead of hearing, "How wonderful, thank-you so much," they heard, "My turkey last year was bigger. I bet management saved the really good turkeys for themselves." "Why'd they give the turkeys to us at work? They should have had them delivered to our homes."

There was no glow of appreciation. Management was hostile, saying, "Those ingrates. We'll never do turkeys again."

During the summer of the following year, the employees formed a committee to discuss what kind of holiday bonus they wanted this year instead of turkeys. There was a faction that wanted holiday hams, a faction that wanted fruit baskets, and a faction that wanted money. Management heard about this committee and waited with trepidation. Late in August, committee representatives sat down across the table from management to negotiate what they would accept as a bonus.

On their side of the table, management was wondering *How did this happen?*

The answer is pretty simple, actually. Bonuses have an insidious way of becoming entitlements. People don't view a bonus as a one-time event; they view it as something that should get larger, larger, and larger.

Don't fall into this trap. Structure pay increases on performance. It has certainly worked for us. The techs who were not motivated to perform have gone elsewhere. The ones who thrive on performance are being rewarded for their efforts. The number of service calls we're performing is up. Customer satisfaction is up. Employee morale is up. You can feel the organization hitting on all cylinders.

There's another area where three is good to go. It's also an area where we challenged conventional thinking and improved customer satisfaction through sound thinking.

I call it the "Tripod." It was a program of work to reinvent the service we deliver.

It's based on two misconceptions. The first is a customer misconception. Most customers call us to *fix* their HVAC. The problem is that nothing is fixed anymore. It's replaced. Think about your automobile. When you take it to the dealer, do they *fix* it? No, they replace the part that has gone bad with a new part. Well, the same is true for HVAC. It has become less expensive to replace the part than it is to try and repair something that's worn or bad. So the service tech's skill is in knowing how to determine what part has gone bad and how to replace that part. Again, like a car dealership, we use diagnostic tools to determine the problem. So from a technical standpoint, what our tech has to be able to do is put the replacement part in correctly.

The second misconception comes from the service companies themselves. They (and we used to be included in this group) believe they sell technical knowledge. They see themselves as a technical business and believe technical is important, so they focus on that.

Because of the way equipment is manufactured and the advanced diagnostic tools available, these companies are putting way too much attention on technical knowledge. It's still important, but it's less important than it was five years ago, and it is much less important than it was ten years ago.

So what is important? Well, you need a system for running the diagnosis, identifying the problem, and replacing the part. We made this an initiative and built a formal process around it that all of our service techs follow. Religiously.

Equally important is explaining to the customer what's wrong, how long the replacement process will take, and why the cost is what it is.

Of third importance is technical knowledge.

I view the three—systems, customer relations, technology—as the legs of a Tripod. You have to have all three or the Tripod's going to crash to the ground.

Obviously, I've prioritized the order differently than other HVAC companies would. And I've done that by viewing the experience from the customer's point of view.

The customer wants to be able to trust the service tech. That's foremost in his or her mind. Trust is something that's developed by building a relationship. And that relationship is created as the tech explains what he's about to do and calms concerns about cost. Of course, things like a well-pressed uniform, keeping a neat work area, and wearing shoe booties help. But it's really the conversation between the tech and the customer that builds trust.

The tech's confidence and the customer's trust are strengthened by the systematic way in which he works. This job isn't about wielding a wrench anymore. We diagnose the same way the techs do at the Apple store's Genius Bar. The biggest difference is that we come to you.

I view both of these legs of the Tripod as relationship builders. The third leg, technology, is mechanical aptitude. Our guys have this in spades. They think through the process, visualize and understand it, do a diagnostic check with a computer, and meticulously replace the part.

Since we instituted the Tripod, customer service ratings have been 95 percent or better.

Put successful initiatives like performance pay and Tripod in place, and you will transform your company. I have to say, both have made us more people centered.

LOOK AHEAD

❏ Make a list of areas within your company that you think could benefit from improvement. Prioritize that list and put together a work plan for tackling the top three.

❏ Is there a person in your company tasked with process improvement? Designating someone to perform this function will make improvements a reality. Process improvement needs a parent to nurture it, gain buy in, and create a successful implementation.

❏ Is your company still a legacy company? How would the change to a meritocracy improve your employee performance? Who would most benefit from the change?

❏ By looking at your service from the customer's point of view, can you reverse engineer your process to make it more customer friendly?

❏ Have you done a customer satisfaction survey? If not, we'd recommend you do one and use it as a baseline. If you have a baseline survey, have you identified the areas of potential improvement?

Birth to Death:
The Business Life Cycle

Pull Theory and the art of pulling your business forward isn't just an interesting management philosophy. It's way more than that. It's about immortal life.

Yes, you heard me right, immortal life. As in living forever.

Businesses, like people, have life cycles. There's birth, growth, maturity, decline, and, gulp, death.

BIRTH

Businesses are born every day. An electrician hangs out his shingle. A florist signs a lease for a storefront. A builder starts his first market home. Those are heady days, where the sky seems limitless and the possibilities endless. Some of those businesses will survive; some will be history before their first *birth*day.

GROWTH

Let's say that electrician who hung out his shingle starts doing the electrical work for the builder who now has two market homes under construction. The electrician has enough work now to add a second electrician. Word gets around that this electrician is good, and he becomes a sub for a larger builder. He adds two more electricians and an office manager. His business is in classic *growth* stage.

MATURITY

Jump ahead twenty years, and the electrical company now employs twelve electricians, four office workers, and handles the business of five builders plus individual customers. The owner thinks the business has grown as large as it can for him to manage by himself. This is a *mature* business—one that has grown, become established, and reached a level or size with which the owner feels comfortable. Remember this, it will become important shortly.

DECLINE

One of the electrical company's homebuilders decides to use a different electrical firm. Four electricians and one office worker are let go. Three other electricians leave shortly after to open their own business. The owner, getting on in years, no longer has the energy to rebuild. Morale and income are in a downward race. These are classic signs of a company in *decline*.

DEATH

The electrical company loses two of the remaining builders. To survive, the owner needs to immediately rightsize the business, but doesn't. The company takes on more and more debt, the bank calls the note, and the owner has no choice but to close his doors, signaling the *death* of his business. RIP. Like the human life cycle, the business life cycle is inevitable. There's no memorial listing the names of traditional business that have died. But here are the names of some businesses you'll recognize: Hollywood Video, Builders Square, Best Products, Musicland, Linens 'n Things, Circuit City, K.B. Toys, Border's Books and Music. All of these promising businesses went through the stages of birth, growth, maturity, decline, and death. Some of those deaths were fast, some were long and drawn out. Fast or slow, a business death is always painful.

With knowledge, however, you can stave off the grim reaper. Death doesn't have to happen. That immortality I promised is possible. Remember when I asked you to remember maturity? Maturity is where rot usually sets in.

Most traditional companies—let's continue using our electrical business as an example—are single service businesses. Being a single service supplier leaves you vulnerable in the marketplace in a number of ways:

- There could be a surge of young, aggressive electricians cannibalizing your business.

- A mega electrical company could enter your market.

- Electrical technology could change, creating less demand for what you do.

- Population shift could move work outside your service area.

Any or all of these could take a mature business and move it into decline. Besides market factors, the owner's actions or inactions can also initiate decline:

- The owner decides he's worked hard all his life, and it's time to take it easy.

- With a short runway until retirement, the owner does little.

- The owner allows the next generation to run things and provides only minimal supervision.

In this case, what we have is a confluence of business and human life cycles. The owner as a young man worked hard to grow his business. As his business matures and he enters middle age, he doesn't want to work as hard. As he eases back, the business starts to decline.

AVOIDING DECLINE

Our scenario with the electrician assumes he's *pushing* his employees, and as he ages he doesn't push as hard so the business declines. But what if he shifted from push to Pull? What if the employees were *pulling* the company forward? Under this scenario, there's no need for the business to go into decline. The young turks keep the place busy and the business viable. The owner could even go to Florida for the winter and the business wouldn't lose a step.

Letting the employees pull the company staves off decline. But even letting a business plateau at its maturity stage is dangerous. It doesn't take much to tip it toward decline.

That's why it's good to look at complementary services that could move the business back into a growth mode. What if the owner of the electrical company added a home appliance service? Suddenly all his eggs aren't in the one basket. Multiple service offerings may give the company a competitive advantage in the marketplace and strengthen his relationship with the company's customers. Most important, it gives the firm a growth venue—a way to move upward off the maturity plateau. And what if the owner hires a young hotshot determined to make her mark, lets her pull this part of the business forward, and the company enjoys rapid growth? The owner may have nurtured someone who will eventually buy the business from him, carrying it far into the future.

Is this immortality? Your call. But it's sure a lot better than watching a business rot and wither away.

LOOK AHEAD

❏ On a piece of paper, plot the business life cycle: birth, growth, maturity, decline, and death. Circle the one that best describes the state of your business. If you selected growth, what will it take for you to keep growing and not plateau into maturity? If you circled maturity, what will it take for you to avoid slipping into decline? What added service offerings could put your company back in growth mode?

❏ Owners: How long is your runway? Is retirement causing you to think short term versus long term? How is this impacting your business?

❏ What's your exit strategy? Do you want to simply close your doors? Wouldn't you rather sell a growth business to a next generation family member or young hotshot?

15

Overwhelmed

There's a question consultants always want to know the answer to: "What keeps you up at night?" When I first contemplated the transformation that was needed at Apollo, my answer was, "What doesn't keep me up at night?" I worried about what needed doing, what I should do first, how I should do it, what I'd do if it didn't work, what people would think, how it would turn out, and so on.

Talk about head trash. I was overwhelmed. The transformation that we needed was too big. I was bogged down with inertia and didn't know how to get past it.

If you're contemplating making a major change to a traditional business, you may feel these same anxieties. In fact, you wouldn't be normal if you didn't.

Nonetheless, that inertia of starting a transformation is something you'll have to overcome. What worked for me was breaking the larger situation into a whole slew of smaller tasks. Once again, I started with the future.

My first step was to visualize the company one year from now, three years from now, and five years from now. At each of these future dates, I documented in detail how I saw the company structured, staffed, and performing. I also documented changing market conditions, competitors, and other potential threats.

Because most of us are visual people, I began laying out my thoughts schematically. The format was simple:

YOUR COMPANY

Staffing:

Structure:

Services:

Performance:

IN ONE YEAR

Staffing:

Structure:

Services:

Performance:

IN THREE YEARS

Staffing:

Structure:

Services:

Performance:

IN FIVE YEARS

Staffing:

Structure:

Services:

Performance:

Obviously, you'll want to choose your own categories and make this schematic a good fit for your needs. I suggest you start with your current situation. Populate it with as much detail as possible. Only by using rigor in your visualization and in documenting the areas of change will you find value in this exercise.

Next, tackle year one, year three, and year five. I think you'll find initiatives in year one may lead you to insights about year three and ultimately year five. Once you have year five completed, do an assessment by category of whether this is where you want your company to be. If the answer isn't to your liking, fill in the more appropriate information and do a work back to see what needs to happen to make that a reality.

One company I assisted in this process did their workup on huge whiteboards that covered three sides of the room. Teams would come in, make additions and deletions, and refine the visualization. At the end of the day, each board was photographed to capture a record of that iteration. Their process lasted three weeks as various groups contributed content. It was fascinating to see the data various groups added.

If you don't have whiteboards, don't let that deter you. You can cover a room's walls with big sheets of paper. Any office supply store will have pads of this paper—some are like giant Post-it notes, which really makes the setup easy. Just make sure you're not using ink that will bleed through to the walls underneath.

After your visualization, once you've populated as much data as possible, begin the task of prioritizing which initiatives will be most beneficial in year one, year three, and year five. Remember, some initiatives may serve as stepping-stones to others. Make sure you identify these key changes. I use a color-coded system: Red indicates a high structural priority, green is a priority for the financial health of the company, and orange indicates a key staffing priority.

Earlier, I talked about having three initiatives going at any given time. Those initiatives should be taken from this list. Our move from legacy to incentive pay, for example, was our number one orange initiative.

These initiatives vary in the amount of implementation time needed. Some take six months and require extensive research, outside counsel, and legal filings. Others can be accomplished in less than two weeks.

Conventional thinking says you should start with the one that will have the most impact on the organization. I suggest you question that because it might be one of the longer and more complicated initiatives to implement.

Sound thinking says you should start with some of the simpler ones. Get a few relatively easy initiatives under your organization's belt. This will give the company a sense of accomplishment and success. That's important, because . . .

With any change, no matter how small, expect naysayers:

"I don't know why he had to change that. It was working just fine."

"He doesn't understand how much more work he's making for me."

"This place isn't as good as it used to be."

Everything you do will be second-guessed, critiqued, and denounced. Even if it goes exceptionally well, you should expect some negative comments.

If you're thin skinned or not confident in what you've started, they'll pounce. Often, that happens on Friday afternoons.

If you have employees who have a work-related problem or are disgruntled in any way, expect a Friday visit. They have carried that monkey on their back for much of the workweek. Are they going to take that monkey home over the weekend to care for it and feed it? No way. They want to drop it off with you and go home without a care in the world. So expect an earful. And understand that if the monkey jumps to your back, that person has taken advantage of you. You've enabled them to walk away from their problems. As word spreads, you'll have monkeys for houseguests every weekend.

Don't accept that. Be firm. Offer assistance, but insist that your employees take responsibility for and resolve their problems. Don't get sucked in. It will just add to your feeling of being overwhelmed. You have to be a rock. Let nothing rattle you. Remember, you are the one with the singular vision and mission.

You are also the one with your foot on the accelerator. Don't be afraid to increase the speed if you judge that the organization is tolerating change well. The more quickly you can accomplish items on your list, the faster you can propel the company forward.

I've seen three successful initiative methods in action at traditional businesses. Each has its own advantages and disadvantages, and you have to decide which way would provide the best environment for your improvement plan. Remember, the subject matter of initiatives differs; you don't have to apply the same method to all. Mixing it up may work better for you.

THE THREE METHODS

1. **Keep the plan to yourself.** This method works best if the organization has significant cliques or factions that might use your initiatives as ways to gain an advantage over their rivals. In this case, you don't want to give them ammunition. Rather, keep your own counsel and try to depoliticize what you're about to do.

2. **Involve your management team.** If you are contemplating changes to the frontline people or processes, gaining buy-in from the management team will go a long way toward making your initiatives succeed. Strong management cohesion will show the company you're serious about implementation. Key managers may act as team leaders for initiatives in their area.

3. **Involve all your employees.** If you can get the whole organization behind your effort, that's huge. If you consider this path, think of it as a two-stage rocket. Get your management team on board first; then involve the entire rank and file.

While I've offered three methods to consider, there are all sorts of others, and one of those may fit you better. Trust your gut on this. Go with the one that feels the best.

Be sure to stay actively involved in whatever initiatives you implement. Employees have a way of hijacking initiatives and changing them to suit their own purposes.

I heard a story about timesheets that's a great example. A company I know that uses timesheets to track billable hours decided to simplify the billing categories. Sounds sensible, right?

They created a committee of three to review the old billing categories and recommend new ones. Two of the employees on the committee decided they could simplify their areas down to just two categories—making it super easy for them to fill in their timesheets each day. The problem was that this didn't give enough detail for billing. When the company president realized the potential billing problems, he rejected their recommendation and sent them back to the drawing board. This time, however, they were disgruntled and sabotaged the process at every turn.

Again, during this crucial implementation period, you can't waver. Not even a little. You will be tested and will need to keep your support strong. This snipping and sniping gets old and can be overwhelming. It will continue until employees see you're not going to be swayed.

LOOK AHEAD

❏ Create a one-year, three-year, and five-year visualization for your company. At each year mark, what are the initiatives that would make the most impact? What are the ones that will give you early implementation success?

❏ Who within your organization could you involve to broaden the visualization or implementation process? Remember, although you have to lead, this isn't something you have to do alone.

❏ What are the "watch out fors" in your organization? Are there land mines you need to defuse before you can launch a series of initiatives?

❏ Try to gauge the level of acceptance for change within your organization. While three has been the magic number of initiatives for us, your organization may tolerate more.

16

R (relationships) + or − V (value) = $ (profit)

Earlier we talked about the service techs building the relationship at the point-of-sale. The same holds true for our installers; they're also responsible for relationship building.

Those relationships are our most important asset. And in reality, it's the only thing we really control.

Apollo has no control over manufacturers. They determine what kind of products they offer and how those products will be built.

Apollo has no control over how those products function. We can't change the specs or alter the performance.

What we can control is how we service those products. Period. The quality of our service determines the value we provide and the relationships we build with the consumers.

Relationships are the R part of the equation. The greater the value Apollo provides, the stronger our relationships with our customers. Weaken those relationships, and Apollo's value diminishes. So the relationships that the service tech or the installation team creates have the ability to take our sales up or down.

Relationships (R) never stay static. They're a constantly shifting area of concern. To make sure it's moving up and not down, we reorganized our company into business units and invested heavily in training. No, not the technical training I warned you about. We invested in relationship development—ways to have better rapport with our customers and have our service fit better with their lifestyles.

To make sure we stay responsive to the customer, we divided the company into four business units: Service, Installation, Maintenance Contracts, and Finance.

Each of these units has short- and long-term goals and benchmarks that must be met. The chief benchmark is customer satisfaction. Part of the thinking behind going to individual business units was to move management closer to the customer. By doing this, we have quicker response and shorter approval times. If there are problems—and no matter how well you run your business, problems will come up—I want them resolved quickly. Each of our managers has the authority to do that.

R not only drives the way we're structured but also determines the kind of training in which we invested.

Our managers received executive leadership coaching. Conventional thinking says this kind of training is beyond what's needed. I disagree. Managers are essentially running their own businesses. I wanted them to feel comfortable making decisions and confident in motivating the people who work for them. That's leadership. It's one of the hardest things to develop, but once it grabs hold, the impact is enormous. It allowed our managers to bring the systems and processes to life for the frontline people with the positive power of Pull.

Extending Pull all the way through our organization to the frontline people was a huge win. To go back to my rowing analogy—for the first time, the entire company was pulling together. There wasn't an oar out of sync anywhere.

I'm confident this synchronized pull will continue. Our meritocracy system compensates managers and frontline staff for performance.

For the frontline people, we've invested in personal development and communications training. Nine times out of ten, if we have a problem, it's because we didn't communicate clearly. Either we didn't set expectations well or we failed to answer questions completely.

Relationships drive value (V) in professional and personal lives. If the individual spends enough time creating relationships through emotional deposits, then that value either increases or decreases as an outcome. Not meeting customer expectations or failing to answer their questions adequately can stem from a lack of personal confidence or from poor communication skills. Doesn't matter. It's a −V in the equation. By providing ongoing relationship training, we've shifted that to +V status.

In +V mode, our service techs are bonding with our customers, giving them valuable information about operating and maintaining their HVAC systems. That "box" in the basement or attic is a mystery to most folks and a headache when it doesn't function properly. It's amazing how much pride of ownership develops for that box when customers understand how to operate it for optimum comfort and energy usage.

If there's a less expensive way to fix a problem, our techs will share that information with the customers. We want them to have confidence that what we're recommending is in their best interest. That's the way you build trust. Then, when big problems come along, the customers know we're on their side. It's all about the relationship.

R means we're in it for the long haul. In the trades, conventional thinking says revenues are measured by what happens during the year. Sound thinking says that R determines revenue and that the real way to measure revenue would be over the life of the relationship. We've studied our relationships and found that many of them are for twelve to fifteen years. (We're proud of that and thankful to our customers. We recognize they have many choices and we're honored they've stayed with us.) Over that same period of time, we know the value of those relationships to the company is between $12 to 15 thousand each. Why so much? Well, over that lengthy time frame, chances are good there's been a full HVAC system replacement, plus ancillary products and maintenance.

Again, the costs are not unlike a car. There are operating, acquisition, financing, and maintenance costs. Our goal is to add value at each step in the process.

There's one other important facet of R. Consumers share the word on which tradesmen are good and bad. If you have good relationships with your customers, they are likely to recommend you to family and acquaintances. Conversely, if the relationship has soured, the customer will warn anyone who will listen to stay away from you. In this day of Angie's List, Facebook posts, and Twitter tweets, it's easy for negative comments to spread quickly and extensively, souring your reputation. Trust is a fragile thing. It doesn't take much to wreck it. Work hard on R to keep your customers.

Finally, you can't sustain a business if you don't make a profit. However, profit these days has gotten to be a dirty word. Customers equate it to gouging. Part of that feeling comes from the Walmarting of America—where the focus is on how low cost you can go.

At Apollo, we work hard at that. We've cut our prices to the bone. To sustain the business at lower profit margins, we have to look to growing our customer base to survive.

We're confident that by going "all in" on R, Apollo will not only survive, but also prevail.

LOOK AHEAD

❏ Can you create a formula for success in your business?

❏ Would a move to strategic business units help you become closer to your customers? Would it improve response times and make you more customercentric?

❏ What's a customer relationship worth in your business? Try to plot that value over the life of the relationship.

The Elephant in the Room

You're probably wondering *Is he ever going to talk money?* After all, if the money slows to a trickle or stops, a traditional business isn't going to last long. You're on life support. What's worse, your creditors are reaching to pull the plug.

Someone like me can talk about staffing, marketing, customer service, but to an owner under the gun—day in and day out—to come up with cash, that's the issue that takes priority. Until it's resolved, the rest of this stuff is just wishful thinking.

Apollo has been fortunate. During my dad's tenure and now during mine, the company has always been cash positive. We've got a line of credit, but we've never had to tap it. That's a blessing. It gives you the luxury of operating from a better vantage point. I don't have the stresses and strains of trying to lead a cash-strapped organization.

But I've talked to enough owners who are in that position to understand how devastating it can be. What I see, usually, is a business where income and outgo have flipped. Income used to be enough to cover expenses, but for some reason—the recession, bad luck, job losses, incompetence—expenses began to exceed income.

Most traditional business owners believe they can right the ship. Many do. But as the ship takes on water, an owner's attention is diverted to bailing and, whether he or she recognizes it or not, all other aspects of the business start to suffer.

That business is no longer thinking long term. Customers are being pressed to do more business with the company and pay in advance. Suppliers are being strung out. That line of credit from the bank begins to look like a lifesaver. And it is, until the business maxes it out and the bank starts applying pressure for the owner to make payments. Often, the business is quickly $100 thousand or $200 thousand in debt, and even the debt service becomes problematic.

One owner I knew said his wake-up call came when a supplier told him that his product supply would be cut off if his company didn't address its payables. Because the company's line of credit was tapped out, the owner had to give the supplier what little was left on his personal credit card. That's when the owner knew he'd hit rock bottom.

There's no shame in getting in financial trouble. Traditional businesses aren't the only ones who have problems. The heavy hitters—GM, Chrysler, AIG, Citibank—have the same woes.

But I think the pain is more acute in a traditional business, where owners may feel like they have failed their extended business family. Unfortunately, if you're in this situation, this is not the time to feel sorry for yourself. You've got to take immediate action.

GET PROFESSIONAL HELP

Get an objective opinion of your situation. Hire a CPA and find out exactly how deep a hole you're in and where the ground is likely to keep falling away beneath your feet. Once you have the facts and firm footing, you can take the appropriate action.

MANAGE YOUR BIGGEST EXPENSE

In most cases, you can't get out of trouble by delaying the purchase of supplies or cutting back on expense reimbursements. Yes, those actions may help a little. But your biggest expense is salaries. If your business is in trouble, this is the area that will provide the most financial relief.

You have to cut back your staff until it's in line with your income. This will be gut wrenching for both you and the staffers you let go. But lightening the ship may be the only way you can keep it afloat. Figure out how deep the cuts need to be and then do it with one fell swoop. Get it over with. Get it behind you. Begin the climb back to business health.

Don't think it will soften the blow to dribble out the layoffs one or two a week. All that will do is make everyone wonder when the next cuts will be and who will be among them. Morale will fall faster than prices on unsold Halloween candy.

Once you have the cuts behind you, talk with the remaining staff members. Tell them you're counting on their help to rebuild the business. This is a time when people need to pull together for the mutual good.

RIGHTSIZE THE REST OF YOUR BUSINESS

With staffing now in line, rightsize what you can. Can you decrease the size of your fleet? Can you consolidate office space (there's something demoralizing about ten people echoing around in an office that once housed fifty)? While not as important as staffing, rightsizing will bring you additional operating efficiencies.

MAKE THE ROUNDS

With the cuts behind you, make the rounds of customers and suppliers. Go to their place of business if you can. Explain that business difficulties have forced you to rightsize your business but that you've taken decisive action and you feel confident about your future. They'll appreciate you for making the effort to come to their place of business and your honesty in telling them about your challenges.

If you're thinking: *Why should I tell them? They probably won't find out.* Get real. Customers, much less suppliers, sense when there's trouble. And if you don't tell them about it, guess what, your competitors will. Better they hear it from you.

KICK BUSINESS DEVELOPMENT UP A NOTCH

Getting financially fit is a lot like getting physically fit. Cutting expenses is cutting back on calories. And, yes, that will help you lose weight. But the other part of losing weight is the part people don't want to do—exercise. New business development is like exercise. You may not want to do it, but you need to, and like exercise, you need to do it in a way that produces results.

Often, that means hiring a new business development person, taking sales training, or both. You may resist hiring a new businessperson, thinking, *I can sell, some of my employees can sell, so why add an additional salary?* The answer is how well do you sell? How well do your people sell?

Whatever made you good at heating and cooling, plumbing, or whatever your traditional business happens to be was probably more "hands-on" driven than "sales" driven. If you don't love selling, find someone who does. Those people are out there. My suggestion is to look for a Capital T in training. You'll want someone with a lot of social skills, determination, and a desire to prove what he or she can do. Consider putting this person on a modest salary plus a commission or a percentage of the business he or she brings in.

Chances are you haven't had any formal training on how to sell. After all, no one really says, "Hey, my goal in life is to become a salesperson." For most of us, sales is something that's thrust on us when the company needs more income. All of a sudden your boss sits you in front of a phone and tells you to cold-call or sends you to networking events to hobnob and hand out business cards. Seldom is any real business developed through either of these methods. A sales training program, however, can teach you how to reach potential customers, and once you do, show you how to interact with them in such a way that they buy.

The key is this: Customers don't want to be sold; they want to buy.

When you're the customer, you don't want to be sledgehammered into buying, do you? Of course not. But when the untrained go out to sell, that's exactly what happens. We're in such a hurry to "close the deal" that we scare the prospect away.

How do I know it happens this way? Because that's what we did until I had all my guys go through sales training. The transformation was unbelievable. Barbarians became virtuosos. The trainers taught us that sales is a chess match. You need to understand the different moves you can make and you need to understand the moves of your customer/competitor. Once you do, there's no need to wield the sledgehammer. You carefully find your customer's pain and you help him or her overcome it.

When you see your close rate go from 20 to 30 percent or to over 60 to 70 percent and the only change you've made is sales training, you'll know it's been well worth the time you've invested.

A GOOD RULE OF THUMB

The financial situation for every business is different, but I did hear a general rule of thumb that made sense to me. A fellow business owner said that for his business to stay healthy, he follows a 50–25–25 rule:

Of gross revenues, salaries should be no more than 50 percent, expenses should be no more than 25 percent, and 25 percent should go to business reserves and profit.

The number he watches most closely is salaries. His salaries were at 67 percent. He's slowly gotten them down to 53 percent and says that has been a big factor in his return to profitability.

A SECOND GOOD RULE OF THUMB

An adviser of mine once told me that I should divide my time this way: One-third should be spent on business operations, one-third should be spent with customers, and one-third should be spent on new business.

Measure how you spend your time. If you're like me, most of it was in operations. Making the shift to spending more time out of the office might not be easy for you, but customers love it when you pay attention to them—so that's good for business. And the more time you invest in new business, the better your growth potential.

LOOK AHEAD

❑ Take your financials for a year and do a trending analysis. What's moving up, and what's moving down? If you're trending downward in either income or profit, what can you do to reverse this trend?

❑ Compare your percentages to the 50-25-25 rule. How far over 50 percent are you on salaries? What could you do to bring down

SQUIRRELS, BOATS, AND THOROUGHBREDS

that percentage? How would lowering that percentage improve your profitability?

❏ Who does the selling in your organization? Be honest. How much selling are you doing? How much is your staff doing? Do you think your closing percentage is high enough?

❏ What would adding a new business development person mean to your organization? Would it create competition? Or would it take sales to a more professional level? Do you know of a Capital T in training that might be a good new business development candidate?

❏ What would providing sales training to your staff mean to your organization? Interview two sales training organizations and see what they might offer you. If you decide to move forward, don't forget to position this as a benefit (additional training and skills) to your staff. They will be more well rounded in business because of your investment.

Coaching: I'll Take the Under, Not the Over

True story. A friend who had just retired decided to take up golf again. He'd been a decent player in his youth, but a recent outing told him he was beyond rusty. A few lessons were definitely in order.

He found a club pro he liked and had the pro critique his swing. After a morning together, the pro told him, "Here are the five things I want you to work on with your swing. Go play five rounds and come back and we'll see how you're doing."

My friend was a little surprised that after an entire morning together, the pro had only five things to tell him. So he questioned him about that.

The pro's response was illuminating. He told my friend there was a lot he could point out, but a golfer could only work on so many things at once. If he told the golfer a whole bunch of things to fix, it was too overwhelming, and nothing got accomplished. He even had a term for it. He called it overcoaching.

That struck a chord with me. Growing up, I had all types of coaches. There were the ones who were constantly in my face demanding better performance. There were ones who didn't care what I did or even if I showed up. It occurs to me that this is indicative of leadership—you can have too much or too little. So the question becomes: Are you overcoaching or undercoaching?

Now the kind of coaching we're talking about here is not the one-on-one mentoring kind; it's the coach getting the players on the field and shouting instructions. There's an equivalent that happens all too often in the business world—it's called a meeting.

I've talked with business owners about their meetings—I've visited larger $100 million companies and smaller $1 million companies—and no matter the size of the business, three themes seem to surface related to meetings: confusion through communication, hands too tight on the wheel, and not letting the flavors marinate.

- **Confusion through communication:** I found there were common meeting scenarios. Some owners met daily with individual senior managers and once a week with their teams. Other owners held a daily huddle with the entire team. Although the meeting scenarios were different, each group thought there was a lack of clarity about the purpose of the meeting and expressed a sense of confusion about what was actually accomplished.

- **Hands too tight on the wheel:** I also found that when owners don't think the business is responding the way it should, they tend to become more hands on, hold more meetings, and strongly demand better performance. As you can imagine, this quickly leads to burnout.

- **Not letting the flavors marinate:** Often owners don't believe their message is getting through. (In actuality, the message has gotten through, but the team hasn't had enough time to act on it.) Frustrated, the owner holds more meetings, re-spinning the message, and keeping the organization in a state of flux.

Wow, did that open my eyes. Was I guilty of any of these? You bet. I was the master of giving my managers, at any given sitting, a whole slew of things to do (confusion through communication). More than that, I held almost daily meetings to do my favorite thing—coach, counsel, and mentor (hands too tight on the wheel). With the managers, I had a short Monday meeting, a longer Wednesday strategic meeting, and another short meeting on Friday. I was giving them so many things to do, and meeting so often with them, that I wasn't giving them time to implement anything (not letting the flavors marinate). I was guilty of classic overcoaching.

So I backed off. That was hard to do. Meetings were a way to keep my finger on the pulse of the business. Fewer meetings might mean things fell through the cracks. Meeting less was not without risks.

I found myself questioning that paradox of leadership: You have more control when you let go.

Sound thinking prevailed. I saw the benefits of clarity rather than overcoaching. To their credit, the managers stepped up. Where I would have been the one wanting to know the status of a particular thing, in this new "fewer meetings" environment, the meetings we did have became more productive because we were talking about accomplishments, not status.

The other benefit was that by focusing on fewer things in meetings, we tended to go deeper on a given subject. Instead of a superficial look, things got the deeper dive needed for real results.

This was so successful that I was temped to eliminate all our meetings. I didn't because there are also risks to undermeeting. You become removed from the organization, and the longer things go without your involvement, the more irrelevant you become.

You have to find your optimum balance. Ours turned out to be a short weekly meeting and a longer strategic meeting once a month. I realized that even with fewer meetings I still had my finger on the pulse of the business through our employee playbooks that summarize weekly achievement and our ongoing program of customer satisfaction surveys.

The playbooks have proven to be a good working tool. My dad had a simple one that measured four categories. From that, he had a good sense of an employee's weekly accomplishments. I expanded the playbook to measure twelve categories. From that, I have a real measure of what has been accomplished, what hasn't been accomplished, and time spent on task.

Besides the playbook, there's one other method I use to keep my finger on the pulse of the business. It's a business philosophy introduced in the late 1960s. Using it is highly unorthodox but scarily effective.

The philosophy was called "management by walking around" (MBWA). Remember, back in the sixties people worked in private offices, often with their doors shut. Information moved at a snail's pace by today's standards. An executive would dictate a memo, send it off to be transcribed, get it back to proof, make corrections, and have it retyped before sending it off via the interoffice mail. Days, weeks, possibly months would pass as this trickle of information went from worker to management, management to worker . . . on and on.

A radical idea was floated that suggested the management executive leave his office (gasp!), walk around, talk to the rank and file, and find out what was actually happening. Management by walking around was all the rage for a very short time before being relegated to obscure business texts.

You wouldn't think it would make much sense in today's open office environment. Especially when you have instant communication between two parties via email and smart phone.

Here's my twist on management by walking around. I pop my head in an employee's office or cube at an unannounced time with a question: "I saw we only had three installs last week, down from twelve the week before. Why is that?"

Okay, this would probably be more appropriately named ambush management. But hey, does it ever work.

The look in the person's eyes, and his or her demeanor, will tell you more than you'll ever get in an email or over the phone. If the issue is a just a blip on the schedule, you'll see the person answer confidently. If the eyes go wide and he or she starts to stutter, you know you're in trouble.

This is an especially good technique to use with accounting.

I would never use it as a replacement for a weekly review of the P&L, but sticking my head in accounting and saying, "I heard miscellaneous expenses were up 300 percent for the month. That's crazy high. Help me understand why."

A good financial person won't miss a beat. He or she will launch into an explanation that accounts for every last dime. If that doesn't happen for you, I can recommend the name of a good forensic accountant.

Sound thinking says meetings aren't the only way to gain information. Don't be afraid to explore other avenues that help you and your employees stay sharp.

One thing about ambush management: It keeps everyone on his or her toes.

LOOK AHEAD

❑ Using a week as a time unit, plot how many meetings you hold on a recurring basis. How many of these are legacy meetings—in place for years—that have lost their value? How many of these meetings produce marginal results? Adding up the cost of employee time in meetings, how much are these meetings costing you?

❑ Would a scorecard system eliminate the need for some of your meetings? Our scorecards measure twelve different factors. What could a scorecard system do to help you get a gauge of your organization in any given week?

❏ Would conducting a sort of pop quiz help keep your employees sharp? In what areas of the business would it help—or hurt—the most?

Highs and Lows

Running a business is not for the faint of heart. Every two weeks or every month you have to make payroll. Some pay periods you wonder if that's going to happen. There's a ton of regulations with which you have to contend. And there are always troubling people issues. No matter what you do as the head of a company, you can't please everyone.

There's a wonderful quote from modern-day philosopher Bill Cosby: "I don't know the secret to success, but I sure know the secret to failure. It's trying to please everybody."

How true. Every decision you make will be criticized and second-guessed. If you're a sensitive soul, I feel sorry for you.

But there's also an incredible satisfaction to be found as the head of a business. If you believe in being a good steward and in shepherding the company forward, you'll experience the high of highs.

Because Apollo has never had any debt (kudos to my dad), I've never been in a position where I had to deal with asking a bank for a line of credit or having to pay that line back. So I won't speak to contending with debt.

What I'd like to talk about is celebrating the highs and lows together. Too often, something wonderful happens and we barely give it a moment's notice. This is a mistake. You need to recognize milestones, both good and bad. Make them memorable.

Let's get the lows out of the way and finish with the highs.

LOWS

I think the low of lows for me came when I first joined the company. Remember, it was my dad's company, not mine. But I quickly realized nobody cared as much as I did about Apollo. This was just a place they came to for a paycheck. Dad was so focused on running the business, he didn't really notice. This might have given me the first inkling of my Pull Theory. I wanted everyone to care.

This was also the time I got a lesson in petty behavior. We let go one of our service techs over performance issues. This tech had a company van that he also drove home nights. After we talked with him about his performance, he put dead fish under the floorboard before giving the van back to us. You wouldn't believe the smell. It was unbelievably rank. It cost us over $1,000 to get the odor out.

Every company has events like this, and I think they're all the more painful because the people who perpetrate them usually have been well treated by the company.

Use these lows as teachable moments. Get everybody together and say, "We're sorry about Joe. We wish we hadn't had to let him go. If there are problems that are keeping you from performing, talk with us, let us see if we can help. Don't do something mean. That isn't helpful to you or us."

Another low for me is the struggle to pay our frontline people a higher wage. Earlier, I talked about the ceiling customers will pay for HVAC service. It limits what we're able to pay our service techs. I continue to try different ways of increasing what we're able to pay them, but it's a struggle to find something that is sustainable. That's a low. I want these employees to enjoy a better standard of living.

Every company has lows, and some employees love to wallow around in them. It's your job not to let them. Use the lows, but don't carry them with you. Get past them as fast as you can.

HIGHS

The highs are the moments that make it all worthwhile. These are the moments you want to savor for as long as you can. Call people together and celebrate. That's just smart business. People want to feel they work for a winner, and the more events you celebrate, the more that feeling permeates the organization.

When numbers are good, I call an impromptu meeting of the management group and it's high fives all around. Everybody leaves charged up.

We do larger things to get everyone fired up, as well. To raise money for Habitat for Humanity, we launched an internal promotion called "True Grit." As the name implies, it had a western theme and aimed to gauge your fund-raising toughness, partner.

Most companies run a promotion like this at one time or another. Some are successful; some aren't. I believe it's the effort you put into the promotion—in this case the true grit behind True Grit—that made it a success.

To kick it off, I rode a horse to work. This is not easy when your place of business is in a busy industrial section of town. Nonetheless, galloping into our parking lot like Rooster Cogburn with his pants on fire got attention. People got in the spirit. True Grit got off to a great start. By the time it was finished, I'm proud to say we exceeded every expectation. And you know what we did? You guessed it; we got together and celebrated.

If I hear one of the staff has celebrated a milestone, aced a certification, received kudos from a client, been recognized by the community, I get everyone together for a quick congratulations. It just takes a minute, but the good it does lasts so much longer.

A personal high for me has been the relationship I've developed with our young management team. This replaced a personal low of overpaying managers to keep them because they were the owners of Apollo's institutional knowledge.

For the new management team, I recruited people who wanted to make a success of themselves. And who understood that the best way to do that was to make Apollo a success.

Early on, I sat with each of them and said, "Paint me a picture of what you want to do with your life."

One told me, "I want to make a million."

"Tell me how you see that happening," I said, "and I'll help you with it. What's the resource allocation you need?" Coaching, counseling, and mentoring these managers has been a treat.

Another high for me has been working with outside advisers.

I know I don't have all the answers, and the advisory group I've put together gives me different perspectives. Don't be afraid to add outside people to your board. In our case, this outside opinion has challenged the conventional thinking and directed us to smarter ways of doing business.

I mentioned stewardship earlier. As the head of a business, you need to be that moral compass, that good shepherd. I find it extremely rewarding. One of my advisers referred to it as loving your people—giving them your fullest involvement to make their professional and personal lives better.

I've taken that to heart. I love them as much as I can, worry it isn't enough, and vow to love them more tomorrow.

Every now and then, you have a jerk—like the fish guy. But the feeling you get by being a good shepherd gives you something money simply can't buy.

LOOK AHEAD

❑ Do you make time to celebrate? What's your next opportunity to celebrate? How can you make it memorable? (Note: Don't ride a horse to the office if you have client meetings that day.)

❑ Do you view your role as stewardship? How are you being a good steward? What would make you a better one?

Taking the Long View

Here's one other important piece to help you manage the daily drama of highs and lows. I was so intrigued with this thought that I had a calligraphy artist letter it up for me so I could keep it front and center on my desk for all my business dealings. It reads:

The longevity of the opportunity is more important than what happens today.

I hear you thinking, *Really? It's a nice sentiment, but are these words to run a business by?* You bet they are.

I want to win at everything I do. That's my competitive spirit coming out. My wife jokes I'm so competitive that I always want to see the collection plate on our side of church get to the last pew before the other side's collection plate.

Each workday, for me, is a competition to see how much I can achieve. I'm pulling. I'm mentoring. I'm talking with customers.

I'm doing new business development. Even when I've put in a jam-packed ten-hour day, I'm thinking I should be doing more.

On days like that, I look at the card on my desk and remind myself *I need to keep my focus on achieving the company's long-term business plan. It's far more important than putting checks next to more things on my to-do list today than I did yesterday.*

Then there are other times where something consumes my entire day. Recently, I had a key employee resign. Although this was a setback for the organization, that little sign kept me focused that the setback was only temporary. I knew we would regroup and keep moving forward.

I mention this because most of the businesses I see have a short-term mentality. I've seen a number of public companies that are managed only to make the quarterly numbers. It doesn't matter whether it makes sense, whether it's good for the customers, or whether it will make operations harder the next month—these companies do whatever they have to in order to make this quarter's numbers.

Private companies are just as bad. A friend who runs a marketing company manages his business based on the monthly numbers. It's income minus expenses, and if there isn't enough income for the month to be positive, he starts billing like crazy because he doesn't want to have a negative month. To me, that's sort of like saying you have to win every inning of a baseball game. While it's great to win each inning, winning the game is what really matters.

So why don't traditional businesses spend more time looking at the long term? I believe it's because there's so little fat in a traditional business that we're all afraid tomorrow is going to be our last day. And, boy, does that shorten your view.

It takes courage to take actions that will cost you now and may not pay off for several years. These may be the very actions it takes to keep your business competitive, but the short-term cost makes them difficult to swallow.

Technology is a wonderful case in point. Computer systems and the training to use them properly are a major expense. Nobody likes to take that hit and pony up the big bucks. But if your servers are overloaded and your computers are underperforming, you need to look at the longer picture and open that checkbook. Forget about having a bad month, quarter, or even year. Look to the longevity of the opportunity.

Same goes for your trucks. If you have a fleet like we do, you know that trucks need to be replaced and/or have graphics redone. Neither of those is cheap or something you want to do. I could only shake my head as I watched the fleet of one local traditional business start to age. At first, they just looked a bit shabby. Then they looked rundown. Based on a recent sighting, I'd say they're now dilapidated. That's an embarrassment. And let's face it, eventually that's going to cost you business. When I asked the owner about it, he said he had a replacement program of two trucks a year, but with the downturn he hadn't been able to replace those trucks. Now he's going to have to borrow more than he can afford to bring the fleet up to date.

Earlier, we talked about adding complementary service offerings. Again, this takes a longer view. Getting a service offering launched is expense after expense after expense. It might be four months, six months, or a year before you're generating revenue—much less a profit. Yet, adding that service line will diversify your offerings and deepen your relationship with your customer. Three to five years from now, if there's a downturn in your core business, that new service offering may be what keeps your business off of life support.

Finally, take the longer view in hiring. Sure, hiring someone to put out a small fire feels good. It's a quick validation that you're actively managing your business. When you see an ongoing blaze, you don't ignore it. You don't establish a flame-extinguishing committee. You put out the fire. End of story.

Well, sort of end of story.

Let's say you hire a Capital T firefighter with an impressive resume of different fires he has extinguished. He's going to quickly eliminate your problem, but after that what's he going to do? Most businesses don't have enough fires to keep him busy and challenged all the time. So they give him other duties that he may or may not be qualified to perform and that he may or may not like doing. Ultimately, these issues will marginalize his value and limit his long-term productivity.

The best hires for a traditional business, in my opinion, are the Capital T's in training. You'll remember they're the diamonds in the rough—bright, articulate, and eager to make their mark. Capital T's in training, however, need mentoring and time to find their sea legs. They're not going to step right in and give you their best on day one. Long term is another story. They're going to be the employees you count on to pull your business forward. But what about that fire?

With a Capital T in training, I would view the fire as a teachable moment. You can make short work of that fire and mentor your protégé in the process. Sure it takes a little of your time in the short term but, boy, have you helped set up this Capital T in training for the future.

Should you have a little sign on your desk that says, "The longevity of the opportunity is more important than what happens today."?

I'd sure think about it.

LOOK AHEAD

❏ Make a list of ten past decisions you've made that affected your business. Go down your list and determine whether each decision was a short-term or a long-term decision. For those you marked as short term, how would things have turned out differently if your action had favored the long term?

❏ Have you given your CFO the latitude to think long term, or are you limiting him or her to the next reporting period? Within your accounting system, is there a way to look at longer-term financials—year to date (ytd), for example—rather than shorter-term numbers?

❏ Instead of thinking about money first, make a list of the things that would position your company for the future. We talked about technology and trucks earlier. What's on your list? And now that you have that list, how can you find a way to make those things happen?

Inside and Outside

I had a fellow CEO of a traditional company say to me at a conference, "My business has been trending down for the past couple of years and I thought I had to take strong action."

He acted so supremely confident that it made me curious about what action he'd taken.

He leaned forward conspiratorially and said, "I bumped our Yellow Pages ad up to a full page. The business will start rolling in."

I was stunned. Not in a good way. Back in the day when the Yellow Pages was *the* bible of information, that might have worked. Today, fewer and fewer homes have landlines. You want a number? You don't reach for the YP; instead, you Google the company name on your smart phone or computer. I had a bad feeling his larger investment in yellow was only going to lead to more red. As in ink.

The interesting thing was that this CEO was a savvy businessman. He ran a quality shop and was a good mentor to his people. As I talked with him further, I realized he was doing all the inside things right and all the outside things wrong.

Here's what I mean by that. Inside things are all the actions you take to create knowledgeable, motivated employees in an efficient and effective workplace. That takes good staffing, ongoing training, an investment in technology, good business practices, and sound management. That's inside stuff.

Outside things are the marketing efforts your firm undertakes to tell your story and generate a steady stream of new customers. For most traditional businesses, marketing is a mystery. It's part science and part art, and most traditional businesses never understand marketing. Common problems are what kind of marketing to do, how to budget for it, how to do it, or who the firm can trust to effectively do it for them either inside or outside the company.

That's a huge problem because marketing is your connection to new customers. It's your opportunity to grow and make a profit. You can get all the inside stuff right, but if you don't do the outside things right, too, your business won't thrive. In fact, like my CEO friend at the conference, you'll start trending down until one day you decide to close the doors.

I don't want to see that happen. So I'm going to try to take the mystery out of marketing. Let's start by understanding the cardinal rule:

It's not about you.
It's about your customer.

This is tough, really tough. Because you're proud of the business you've built and you want to let people know what a good job your business does. That's why you hear things like, "It's the best checking account in the world," or, "No hospital cares for you as much as we do." These companies say these kinds of things out of pride, and when they do, unfortunately, they're talking to themselves. All that hyperbole gets old pretty quick, and even worse, it's not what customers want to hear. They don't want to hear you talk about how wonderful you are. They want to know how your product will benefit them. For example: "Offering you the most convenient ATMs," or, "More clinical experience for better outcomes."

Giving your customer a reason to choose you is what marketing is all about. But how do you know what appeals to your potential customers? And who are those potential customers? This leads us to the second cardinal rule:

Know your customer.

Getting to know your customer is in the realm of research, and there are many ways to wrestle this bear to the ground. You can do the research yourself. You can have someone in the firm do it for you. You can buy it from a third party. It doesn't matter how it happens. What's important is that it gets accomplished. Because the more you know about who buys your product or service, the better your chances are of gaining new customers.

The best place to start is with your current customers. You probably have the ability to do customer segmentation. This is often just basic information—services used, frequency of use, part of town, method of payment—that you have acquired with each service call or transaction. From this you can begin to build a profile of your best customers:

They do this amount of business with us.

Their average ticket amounts to this many dollars.

They live in these eight zip codes.

They use our services this many times a year.

You're off to a good start. But there's a lot of information missing that it would be good to know. For example:

Is the purchaser male or female?

What's the customer age segment that most consumes our product or service?

What need does our product or service fulfill?

What appealed most to them about us?

What would make them continue to choose us?

What media do they consume?

How did they hear about us?

There are a variety of ways you can gain this additional information. You could:

❏ Conduct a telephone or web survey or send them a short questionnaire.

❑ Call on church groups or school organizations and conduct interviews.

❑ Hire a research firm to do focus groups or mall intercepts.

Start with the method with which you are the most comfortable. Add as much as you can to your customer profile. Ultimately, you want to be able to know with assurance that your best customers are (as an example) women, between the ages of twenty-five to forty-five, who work outside the home. They are married, own homes valued between $200,000 and $450,000, and live in these zip codes. They read these three magazines, listen to these two stations on drive-time radio, and watch the late evening television news.

Why should you be interested in building this profile? It's because your best prospects will be very similar to your current best customers. If you have a good profile of who's currently doing business with you, you can target those most likely to become customers. By doing this, you're not trying to appeal to everybody (something that always leads to failure); you're focusing your limited marketing resources on the areas with the greatest potential.

You've also gained some important insights into where to advertise because you know the magazines these women read, the general time they listen to the radio, and the time they watch TV.

Okay, you've just had a crash course in Marketing Research 101. Now it's time for your homework assignment.

LOOK AHEAD

❑ Begin to build a profile of your best customers. Use all the information you can pull from your internal systems. Begin to personalize this information by finding pictures in magazines that illustrate these demographics and bring your customers to life.

❑ Once you have a profile of your best customers, consider building additional profiles. Who are your least profitable customers? Who are customers who would do more business with you? What customer groups would you like to add? What's the customer profile of your biggest business competitor? How would what you've learned from profiling help you attract these customers?

❑ Compare your customer data with that of any trade associations to which you belong. How are your customers similar or different from those of the association?

Three Rights for Success

Now that you're looking at things from the customer's point of view and have profiled your best customers, you're armed and ready to go after new customers.

Here's the good news: Do three things right and you'll have huge success. What are those things?

Say the right things, in the right place, at the right time.

Here's the bad news: This is a zero sum game. Get any one of the three wrong, and potential customers don't know you exist.

Let's go back to my CEO friend from the conference who supersized his Yellow Pages ad. Was he in the right place? He certainly thought so. But what about all those people who don't have a landline and don't have the Yellow Pages in their homes? They'll never see his ad. He might have done better running a series of Google ads. Advertising where your customers will see it is crucial.

You've undoubtedly noticed that two of the three "rights" have to do with media. That's because getting your message in front of prospects is *that* important. Think back to the customer profile we created. We determined that your customers read these three magazines, listen to these two stations on drive-time radio, and watch the late evening television news. Because your best prospects are very similar to your best customers, we know multiple media vehicles that are *right places*.

Okay, now we know the right places. What's the *right time*? Seasonality may enter into this. At Apollo, we know when our peak heating and cooling periods are. We also know that plumbing can happen any time. So for heating and cooling, we start marketing before the season kicks off. For plumbing, we have a presence year round.

This leads us to what's the *right message*? Here's where it starts to get complicated. With messaging, you have two levels to worry about—what I'm going to call brand messaging and transactional messaging.

It's easy to explain with an example. BMW's brand message is "The Ultimate Driving Machine." Their transactional message is "Right now, you can get a BMW with zero down, zero first month's payment, and zero APR." The brand message makes you want it; the transactional message gives you the incentive to buy *now*. Again, you need to do both to optimize your business potential.

Creating a brand message is the more difficult of the two because it requires you to say in a few well-chosen words why you are unique. I say well-chosen words because they need to set a tone or create an image. Imagine if BMW had used "The Ultimate Driving Automobile." It doesn't have the same oomph, does it?

As you think about what your brand message might be, steer clear of what others in your market have used, as well as things that are overused.

If someone in your market is using "Service in an Hour," don't try to use "One-Hour Service." You'll sound like you're copying the other company. Instead, go in a different direction, such as, "We Have the Most Highly Trained Technicians."

Some themes are so overused they become meaningless. Think how many times you've seen traditional companies advertising "You Can Trust Us," "We're Your Trusted Source," or "We Earn Your Trust Every Day." No one can really own the attribute of trust. So don't try. Find a way to demonstrate it rather than say it. "We Do It to Your Complete Satisfaction or It's Free."

Developing a brand message is a task that requires a good deal of thought. Even the best ad people don't strike gold in the first five minutes. Maybe not even in the first five days. If you decide to tackle this job yourself, make a list of your thoughts over a period of weeks. Take the best of those thoughts and try to make a short list of, say, three brand statements. Research those three and see which one gets the best response. You can find out using a simple survey. Show the three statements to friends. Show them to a church group. You'll learn a lot by their reactions. And if you don't get a good response, no harm done. Try your hand at a second round. Like many things, you get better at this the more you work at it.

Transactional messaging is much easier. You're offering the customer an incentive to act now. So if you were using "We Have the Most Highly Trained Technicians" as your brand message, your transactional message might be "Get the Top Techs Without Paying Top Dollar. Act Before (This Date) and Save 10%."

The point of brand messaging is to differentiate your product or service in the mind of the consumer. This is a message you're going to want to stick with and build over time. Transactional messaging is designed to make the cash register ring. Many of the big consumer and package goods companies have multiple offers in test at any time. If one doesn't resonate with the consumer or give the company the lift they're looking for, they try another. So don't be afraid to change transactional messages and offers.

LOOK AHEAD

❏ Make a list of brand messaging you like. What is it that appeals to you about the themes you've chosen? Is there a common element in these themes? Can you build on that appeal or common element in coming up with your brand messaging?

❏ Make a list of all your competitors' brand messaging. Begin dissecting their messaging to see what they view as their main strengths. Is one trust? Is another quick service? If so, these are areas you should avoid or find a more creative way to take this position.

❏ Develop ten brand messages for your product or service. Put each on a piece of paper and hang them on a wall. Over a period of a couple of days, does one of them stand out to you? Is there one you don't like as much? Begin to create a short list. Don't be afraid if an idea strikes you to add another message to the wall. Invite people into your office; get their reactions.

❏ Develop five transactional messages. Remember, these should cause the consumer to act now, so there must be an act-by date contained in the messaging. Limited time offers require some disclaimer copy. If you don't know what this should be, consult an attorney, contact your Better Business Bureau, and study what others in your field are using.

Laws of the Jungle

In one of our marketing meetings I was being my usual disbelieving self. Out of frustration, the marketing team began explaining things in terms of laws of the jungle. It worked for me. I repeat them here because they may work for you also.

FIRST LAW: IF YOU WANT TO MATE . . .

Jungle animals know that if they want to mate, they have to stand out. Whether it's rhinos, lions, or chimpanzees, the males of the species know they have to dazzle the females. The same is true in marketing. If you run an ad that looks just like the ads for all your competitors, you don't stand out. And if you don't stand out, your chances of having the consumer choose you are greatly diminished.

SECOND LAW: IF YOU WANT TO EAT . . .

A great many jungle animals hunt in packs. With more animals on the hunt, there's a better chance they'll capture prey. The same is true in reaching consumers. Using one media is like hunting solo. You want to reach the consumer in multiple places. So plan to use a combination of print and electronic ads, possibly even some radio or TV.

There's a second aspect to the Second Law: The more ads you run (media buyers call this frequency), the more success you'll have. Don't think you can run one radio spot one time and everybody will hear your message. Reach consumers multiple times with your message, and that message will begin to register.

THIRD LAW: IF YOU WANT TO SURVIVE . . .

Survival in the jungle isn't easy. Overcoming harsh conditions, multiple predators, and the intrusion of man takes constant vigilance. Animals must pay attention to scents, sounds, and instincts to quickly escape danger. As marketers, we must pay constant attention to market conditions and nimbly adjust our marketing to make sure we not only survive but also prevail. The media vehicle that worked for you last year may not generate any leads this year. Measure every media vehicle by its performance in the marketplace.

FOURTH LAW: IF YOU WANT TO BE FEARED . . .

In the jungle it's threaten or be threatened. The bigger beasts are able to intimidate smaller scavengers and even some bigger animals. The same is true in marketing. The company that "muscles up" and dominates is the one that will intimidate other companies. You can be that dominant company by making sure your marketing is in the right place, at the right time, with the right message. Do that and you've relegated your competition to second-tier status.

Maybe the jungle thing is kind of juvenile; still the points are good. They hold true both for your marketing and for your business in general. In fact, when you combine them with something else my marketing people taught me—"An ounce of innovation in the product is worth a pound in the promotion"—you might really be able to create a sizable advantage for yourself.

Let me give you an example of what I mean. There's a traditional business with a fleet of trucks, and each truck is wrapped in hot pink. You can't miss them; they seem to be making deliveries everywhere. This is a great demonstration of the First and Fourth Laws of the Jungle. By making their trucks stand out, they're drawing attention to their brand. Because they're so noticeable and you see them so often, they seem to dominate all the competitive fleets. What's even better . . . when you do something like this, you absolutely drive your competition crazy.

Another traditional business owner I know invested heavily in a celebrity spokesperson and bought a media schedule of TV, print, and outdoor. He admitted it was a stretch financially, but he thought his customer base was aging and he needed to bring on new customers. He was using the Second and Third Laws, for sure. So how did he do? The campaign ran for three months with no real uptick in business. He began to panic. At the six-month point, he saw his first increases and began breathing easier. By the end of the first year, he was up 9 percent. Continuing the campaign in year two, his business rose 14 percent. His investment was more than repaid.

Here at Apollo, we've applied all four laws. While our trucks aren't shocking pink, in keeping with the First Law, they are bold and graphic. We've evolved our techs' uniforms to make them look more professional, less wrench monkey. Our marketing reflects the Second Law. We use multiple media vehicles, electronic advertising, print, radio, and outdoor to reach our existing and potential customers. And we have enough frequency that we reach folks multiple times. I just love it when someone says, "I see your messages everywhere." Law Three was the easiest one for me. I like to shake things up. Only now I do it based on our changing consumer profile. Law Four, believe it or not, is the hardest law to judge. But our yearly sales increases tell me that we have to be doing a lot of the right things right.

LOOK AHEAD

❏ How can you stand out in your marketplace? Do you have an opportunity to do so with your building, your fleet, your trucks, or your marketing?

❏ We all fall back to the things that worked for us in the past. But what worked for you in the past may not work for you now. What are the new ways you should be reaching potential customers?

Remember, reaching them through multiple vehicles increases your effectiveness.

☐ Is there a way you can dominate in your marketplace? One company I know advertises in every church bulletin. What could you do that would increase your profile? Remember, consumers like to work with companies that look stable and successful.

24

Do It Yourself? Or Hire an Agency?

Marketing is a talent business. By that I mean it's like throwing a baseball or playing the piano.

There are people who can throw 100 mph fastballs. There are people who play Beethoven at Carnegie Hall. Those things take talent.

Me, I can't play "Chopsticks." And I'll be the first to admit I stink at marketing. I'm really an operations guy at heart. If you're like me and have no aptitude for marketing, you might want to consider hiring a marketing firm to do it for you.

Hiring an agency can be boom or bust. I've known traditional companies (including ours) who have had very positive long-term agency relationships. I've also known CEOs of traditional companies who get red in the face as they rant and rave about how multiple agencies have "screwed them over."

I can tell those last three words have you cringing, thinking *I don't need that.* But before you make that decision, let's do a deeper dive on doing it yourself versus hiring an agency.

DO IT YOURSELF: PROS AND CONS

If you choose to do marketing yourself, you as CEO can wear the marketing hat, you can designate a staffer to handle these duties, or you can tag team the task. I'd advise the latter. As CEO, you should be the one who sets the marketing direction and makes sure everything stays on message. That said, you shouldn't be spending your leadership time writing coupon copy. So finding an associate who can take responsibility for the day-to-day advertising tasks is a smart move.

By keeping marketing internal, you eliminate the cost of an agency. As a budgetary line item, your expenses will be lower. You will still need to buy the marketing tools and training—computers, photo libraries, etc.—that you'll need.

You'll find the media (newspapers, radio, coupon books) will be only too happy to make proposals as to what you can expect if you advertise with them. Some will even give you free—that's right, free—production services. They'll prepare an ad or allow you to use a station announcer to voice a spot. This can be attractive because it allows you to get a message out with a minimum expenditure of time and money. *Caution*: You get what you pay for; these people have no real interest in your success. They're only interested in selling ads or time. Your ad or radio spot will be put together quickly with little thought. Chances are, you'll look or sound like everyone else. You won't stand out.

You can also contract with the media but produce your own materials. In this scenario, you create the offer, write the copy, lay out the ad, and forward it to publication. Depending on the talent of your internal staff person, the end result might be outstanding or it might be an unmitigated disaster. A staffer at a traditional business here in town put together an ad that had two misspellings in the headline and a photo that got squished so the two-story house portrayed looked like it had been stepped on by a giant. Another traditional business owner decided he could read his own radio copy. "After all," he said with his nose in the air, "car dealers do it all the time. How tough can it be?" He found out the hard way. When his spot aired, he sounded like a remedial reader—slow, flat, awkward—bush-league stuff, pure and simple. If you're going to create ads and broadcast materials yourself, get the training that will allow you to handle the task properly.

Bottom line, if you choose to keep things internal, you'll be frugal but you'll only be marginally effective.

HIRE AN AGENCY: PROS AND CONS

In my dad's day, there were only advertising agencies. Now there are branding agencies, traditional advertising agencies, interactive agencies, social media companies, promotion agencies, and the list goes on. I believe you'll want a traditional advertising agency because they usually have the ability to bring to your table all the resources you'll need.

Choosing an agency is like dating. Chances are you didn't find your spouse on your first date. It took you several meetings and a lot of time together. The same is true for finding an agency partner. Meet with a number of agencies, find the one with which you have the best chemistry, and spend time getting to know those staffers who will work on your business and the kind of creative work those staffers produce.

Like a marriage, it's the chemistry between company and agency that will determine compatibility and, ultimately, long-term success.

And like a marriage, there's going to be drama, fights, and arguments. Expect that. An agency doesn't see your business the same way you do, and that's going to frustrate you both. An agency sees things from the consumer's viewpoint, which is good. If you've done your homework and truly know your customer, then there will be less conflict. You'll be able to evaluate the agency work, accepting it when it's on target and rejecting it when it's not.

You have to be very specific about what you expect from the agency. A friend tells a story that giving her agency a project is a lot like dropping her car off at the dealer for servicing.

She took her car in for 50,000-mile servicing—oil change, tire rotation, lube, and filter. The price should have been $59.99, and the car should have been ready for pickup at the end of the day. The service manager called and said they wanted to check the serpentine belt, which appeared to be cracked. He wanted to know if they could keep the car another day. The owner said okay and, the following day, called to make sure the car would be ready.

Unfortunately, the service manager wasn't in and nobody seemed to know anything, so she left the car there and called the following day. After four calls, she finally reached the service manager who told her, yes, the serpentine belt needed to be replaced and there were several other engine-related issues. When she asked how much this was all going to cost, the service manager said he wasn't sure but that the car should be ready for pickup the following day. The owner wasn't happy, but what could she do? She felt stuck. When she picked up the car—three days later than promised—she was presented with a bill for $1,200 for work she really hadn't authorized.

My friend says beware of agencies that operate this way. You have a single-page ad you need worked up and you receive an estimate for $1,000. You okay the estimate and expect to see the ad in seven working days. When the seventh day passes, you call and learn there are some issues that need to be resolved. A week later, you call again and they're ready to show you your ad. Why are you a little nervous? Probably because when you see it, they've chosen a different subject for the ad, changed the offer, redesigned your logo, and had a photograph taken by a pricey photographer. Total bill: $12,000. Oh, and the money's also due at the publication tomorrow. There's no time to change anything.

This is exactly what scares traditional businesses about agencies. Again, find an agency with which you have good chemistry and this will be kept to a minimum.

Bottom line, an agency will cost you more money than handling things internally. Be prepared to gulp and open your wallet. It's going to be more than you expect or want to pay. But their work will be far more effective and should secure significantly more business for you than your internal efforts.

COMMIT TO MARKETING

Whichever path you choose, you need to commit to marketing for the long term. Don't do one promotion and if you don't get the uptick you want, say, "That was a mistake; we'll never do that again."

A marketing guy shared this story with me that put it all in perspective:

> Advertising is like exercise. When you exercise regularly, you feel good. Of course, exercise is work and there's always something else you'd rather be doing, so you stop going to the gym. A month or two later, you don't feel as good—you feel sort of dull and lethargic. So you decide, hey, better get to the gym and get my energy back. Except this time after you exercise, you don't feel fit; you still feel lethargic. Getting back to feeling good the way you did before you quit exercising will take work and time.
>
> Advertising works the same way. You do it and you bring in a steady stream of customers. You think, hey, I've got all these customers coming. Why do I need to advertise? I'll just bank that money. But the stream of customers starts to slow. To generate more traffic, you start advertising again, but the customers don't flock in right away. It takes time to build that business back—much of which you've lost to your competition.

Commit to marketing. Allow it to build a steady stream of customers and allow it to maintain that stream. Stopping and starting will only hurt your efforts. Many of the leading companies in any market are the ones that have maintained good marketing continuity—whether internally or agency driven. That consistent message tells consumers you're a reliable, stable company.

LOOK AHEAD

❏ Write a short statement of what you'd like your marketing efforts to achieve. Be realistic. Don't say I want to grow my business 400 percent in six months. Set achievable goals. Now put down pros and cons for both handling marketing internally and hiring an agency. Considering what's on your list, who do you think will best accomplish your marketing goals?

❏ Establish a marketing budget for the year. Make this a figure you can live with. Learn what that dollar figure can purchase for you in terms of getting your message in front of potential customers multiple times in multiple places.

❏ Find the internal person that you think might have potential to handle your day-to-day marketing duties. Give this person a project—creating a promotional postcard, for example—and see how he or she does. If you see potential, have a discussion about how handling marketing might fit in with this person's other responsibilities.

❏ Interview a few agencies. Again, this is like a first date. Invite them to your offices to present their capabilities. There's no cost with this (other than that they will call you repeatedly to see if you'll give them your business). These capabilities presentations will give you an idea of what agency people and resources can do for you. Ask about costs. Their honesty in answering those questions will tell you a lot.

❏ If you click with one of these agencies, schedule a second meeting at their offices. This allows you to see their working environment, the people who will be working on your business, and more samples of their work. Ask to see any work they've done for traditional businesses.

The Game Changer

Remember my fellow CEO at the conference who knew he could solve dwindling sales by increasing the size of his Yellow Pages ad? In case you're wondering, it failed. Dismally. Fortunately, his son—an up-and-comer in the business—convinced his dad that what they really needed was a more informative website. The son had friends who built sites and, for not that much money, they were able to develop a more expansive site that gave them an easier way to connect with their customers.

Customers know, before they do business with anyone, they can do research online and find out about the companies from which they can choose. This is true whether consumers are looking for a tree trimmer or a thoracic surgeon. The web is the first place they go.

Speaking of firsts, your website also offers customers their first impression of your business. Unless you've just created or revamped your site in the past two years, it's time to do it again.

This time—whether you do it yourself or have a traditional agency or interactive agency do it for you—think about what you've learned about your customers. Build your website or have it built from your customers' point of view. Take a look at these company website do's and don'ts:

DO

❏ Give them a simple way to schedule a service call.

❏ Give them a way to get an estimate in less than twenty-four hours.

❏ Give them a way to track your technician and learn if the tech is on time.

❏ Provide them with reasons to do business with you.

❏ Put a face on your company. (Nobody wants to do business with an impersonal company.)

❏ Show (if possible) that you work in their neighborhood.

❏ Give third-party testimonials.

❏ List your company on BBB or Angie's List if possible.

DON'T

❏ Make your site text heavy.

❏ Use stock photos that customers may have seen in other places (possibly a competitor's site).

❏ Make consumers go more than two clicks to find needed information.

❑ Create a response mechanism to which no one in your organization responds.

Those don'ts sound so basic, yet you'd be surprised at the number of people who don't do them and build websites that offer a terrible user experience.

A good user experience on your website is crucial. You want consumers to find your site informative and easy to work with. Think of it as a sample of what it will be like to work with your company.

Your website must work on a computer, naturally, but it should also be designed to work on a smart phone. Increasingly, consumers are using smart phones to handle their banking, order a pizza, and yes, even schedule appointments with businesses like yours. Smart phone users are already a fast-growing segment of the population and will grow exponentially in the next few years as carriers cease to offer "dumb" cell phones and force the migration to smart phones.

Think about it. Never before have traditional companies had such an opportunity to be more than a name on a truck and a tech ringing the front doorbell. A well-designed website allows a long-term opportunity to provide consumers with visuals, benefits, and testimonials about your company. Of all the tools in your marketing tool belt, the web is a game changer.

Your website can also be a wonderful recruiting tool. It can give potential applicants a sense that you are the employer of choice in your category, and it can provide a response mechanism for taking that interest to the next step.

LOOK AHEAD

❑ Spend some time surfing the web looking at websites of companies in your category. What are they doing well? What are they doing poorly? How does your site compare with the better sites you see?

❑ Pretend you are a customer. How would you rate your site? Is it easy to navigate? Does it deliver a good user experience? What would give your site a better user experience?

❑ How could your site begin to put a face on your company? Think of the visuals you'd like your customers to see. What kind of an impression does it create? Remember, the first way we evaluate anything is visually.

❑ What kind of functionality would you need to tie your website to your estimating process or scheduling? These are important areas to consumers. How can you make your site more responsive to potential customers?

Rings Around the Bull's-eye

I've been talking marketing, but I'd like to put my operations hat back on for a moment, because getting to know your customers has implications far beyond marketing.

On a whiteboard in my office there's a drawing of a target. You can picture that graphic in your mind. A circle surrounded by four rings. Here's what's different about this particular target. In the center of the circle, written in my almost illegible scrawl, is "heating and cooling."

That's the business my dad nurtured and built and, to this day, it's our core Apollo business.

On the first ring around the bull's-eye I've written the word "plumbing"—a service offering I added just a few years ago.

At the time, I wasn't looking to add another service line. I was up to the logo on my shirt in customer data. And what that data was telling me—almost shouting at me—was that our customers viewed heating, cooling, and plumbing very similarly. Being an operations guy, I knew the logistical support needed for plumbing was already in place. Talk about an ah-ha moment.

I realized we could add a product line and extend and strengthen our relationship with our customers. This is what the heavy hitters do when they have a successful product and suddenly that product name appears on all sorts of related things. Of course, the heavy hitters probably do feasibility studies, write business plans, and do test marketing in selected cities first.

I just figured plumbing made good sense and green-lighted the addition. That's the beauty of a small business. You can make change happen on a dime.

Today, our plumbing business has grown more than 600 percent and contributes a significant revenue stream to our business.

I wouldn't have been as confident about plumbing at the time, if it weren't for our customer profiling. I knew from the data that plumbing would be a hit. Now that it's an established service offering, we're looking at the next rings (that's right, plural) of the target. As we delve deeper into the customer data, what we're seeing is that consumers would rather have one relationship for home system service than two or three or more relationships. That means our customers would likely welcome the addition of electric, security, or even appliance repair. We're actively researching those now.

Adding service lines offers a huge upside, but it also has a downside. Our core business is still heating and cooling. That's what Apollo's customers have come to rely on us for. You have to be careful with service line expansions that you don't go crazy and spread your company resources so thin that you do a poor job with your core business.

I keep that target graphic on my wall as a reminder. I never want to lose sight of our core competency as we fill in more rings.

Be aware that the customer profile you develop may assist you in adding a complementary service, as we did, or it may direct you to other operational improvements.

I have a friend who owns a traditional business that operates a headquarters showroom and three satellite showrooms. Of the three satellites, one was always behind the others in sales. Not enough that my friend ever considered closing the location but enough that it became the company's stepchild.

My friend did a customer web survey and, on the subject of the underperforming showroom, was surprised when he got two almost identical comments:

"The traffic is so bad getting there that I steer clear of that showroom."

"They'd have been smarter to locate it at (name of shopping plaza two miles away)."

He did some further research with employees and customers and heard nothing but complaints about the traffic. While he didn't like what he heard, he knew what he had to do. As soon as the lease was up, my friend packed up the showroom and moved it. He'll tell you that simple change did two things: It improved employee morale and it brought that showroom's numbers in line with the other satellites' sales.

Another fellow traditional business owner was surprised to learn from the employees who worked the sales counter that customers were disgruntled by her company's hours. For over twenty years, her distribution company had kept the same hours—eight in the morning until six at night weekdays, eight to noon on Saturday. After all those years, she saw little reason to change.

Still, it nagged at her. Hers was a customercentric business, and if there was something her customers wanted from her, then she wanted to be accommodating. So she made a few phone calls to customers she'd known for years and shared that she was considering changing her company's hours. Each and every customer told her that was a good idea, but some wanted her company to be open earlier and some wanted it to be open later.

She finished her calls thinking she'd just opened a huge can of worms. But you don't get to be a successful business owner by not having flashes of brilliance. And that's just what struck her as she was waiting at a red light on her way into work the following morning.

She made Tuesdays her early day; the company opened at six and closed at four. That gave the people who needed to get an order filled before they went to the job site time to get that order filled.

She made Thursdays her late day; the company opened at ten and closed at eight. That gave the people who wanted to pick up things at the end of the day the time to do so without leaving their job site early.

Once the new hours were in place, she did an email survey about them to her customer base. Seventy-two percent of her customers responded that the new hours were an improvement. Nine percent said the new hours made them more likely to do more business with the company.

LOOK AHEAD

❏ Based on your customer profile, make a list of the operational improvements that would strengthen your customer relationships.

❏ Try the target exercise. Are there service line extensions that flow naturally from your core competency? What would it take in terms of financial and human capital to make that first ring a reality? What would it take to make the second ring a reality?

Time, Talent, and Treasure

All of us have a limited supply of three precious commodities: time, talent, and treasure. What we do with them is the measure of our lives. This is what a purposeful life is all about.

You need to have a plan for how you're going to spend these three precious commodities. Otherwise you'll fritter them away, look back later in life, and have nothing to show for them.

So here's what I want you to do. Get out a piece of paper, place it in front of you so that it's lengthwise or horizontal, and draw a line from left to right. On the left, at the start of the line, write your birth date. On the right, at the end of the line, write the date of your death. Go ahead, I know you don't want to think about it, but put down what you believe is a likely year.

Now figure out where this year falls on the line and write in that date. Scribble over the line between your birth date and now. That's history. The line between now and your death is what you have left in which to accomplish things.

Sobering, isn't it?

Now I want you to write on that line major events that will occur (kids graduating from college, you retiring, your spouse retiring) or events that you'd like to happen (remodeling the kitchen, selling the business, taking an Alaskan cruise) during that time period. Write in everything, and if that line isn't full of events, ask yourself, why isn't it? This is the game plan for the rest of your life.

TIME

Every day is a miracle you've been granted. Don't waste a single one. Pack in as much living as you can.

I finish each day feeling as though I haven't done enough. The way I look at it, I've traded a day of my life for what I accomplished that day. And if it doesn't feel like enough, then it makes me want to accomplish that much more tomorrow.

Your timeline will show you how much runway you have left. If there are initiatives that will take time—years, perhaps—you'll want to get those going as soon as you can.

I had a friend who was employed by a Fortune 50 company but always wanted to run his own shop. He took a package when he was sixty-four and opened a brick-and-mortar business. What with leases, hiring, and inventory, it took him longer than he thought to get it started and much longer to see it develop into anything. By the time the business was what he'd visualized, he admitted to being too old to enjoy it. Colonel Harland Sanders was certainly successful starting Kentucky Fried Chicken at age sixty-five. I think if Sanders were still alive, he'd agree with my friend that starting a business becomes harder as the runway becomes shorter.

Give some thought to what you want to accomplish. Manage your remaining time well. If you want to visit all seven continents, you can do it. Of course, if you only have two weeks of vacation at a time, you'll need to plan when and where you'll be going over a period of years. It would be very doable with good timeline management.

One important time management tool I learned from Stephen Covey was don't waste precious time on unimportant things. It's easy to get bogged down in email, gossip, or trivia. They're meaningless time wasters that add nothing to your day. Instead, focus on what you must deal with: crises, deadlines, mentoring opportunities, and visualization. These are the things that constitute time well spent. They're things that will pay you dividends when you handle them quickly and efficiently.

Time management is an art. You won't suddenly be a master at it. But if you always keep the thought of limited time and maximum accomplishment in front of you, gradually better time management will become a habit.

TALENT

Talent is the hardest thing to come to grips with. Maybe when you were a kid there were two things at which you excelled: academics and sports. You might have had a talent for math or English, possibly baseball or football. But if you didn't, the concept of talent was foreign to you. More than that, the concept of talent was taken away from you. At some point, you were deemed *average*.

The first time I realized I had talent was when I was listed as the ninth best rower in the United States. Ninth! That was a huge moment. Other people were recognizing that I was not only good; I was the ninth best in the entire United States.

In retrospect, my rowing talent was an easy thing to spot. It was not unlike the ability to throw a baseball 90+ mph or playing Beethoven piano concertos at a concert level.

These are talents that rise up and present themselves. Other talents are much more difficult to recognize, things like the ability to:

Design processes and systems.

Create consensus.

Design new products.

Coach others.

Understand the consumer.

Estimate jobs.

I could go on and on, but you get the idea. Every business needs people with talents that give the company value in the marketplace. Rarely are any of these talents talked about. No one gets recognition at a company meeting for his or her ability to build consensus. But that talent just might play a huge factor in that company's success.

Some of these hidden talents emerge on the job. You might get thrown into the job of designing a process. You've never done that before, but as you work on it, you find you enjoy the work, and the end product turns out to be fantastic. You've just discovered a talent you didn't know you had.

I'm a firm believer that you can become not only book smart but also book talented. A quick search in the business section of any good brick-and-mortar or web bookseller will turn up a book on just about anything. Want to know about search engine optimization? There's a book for that. Want to know about personality profiling? There's a book for that. Want to know about project management? There's a book for that, too.

With a little diligence you can become an expert on just about anything. That knowledge is the next best thing to natural aptitude for tackling and wrestling a task to the ground.

TREASURE

This brings us to our third precious commodity: treasure. For many people, this is what it's all about—the accumulation of wealth. Having the income to drive a Porsche 911 Turbo, live in a 12,000-square-foot McMansion with a pool and tennis courts, fly private planes, and take the kids skiing in Switzerland for spring break. This is conspicuous consumption at its best.

The late Jay Chiat, cofounder of Chiat/Day, the legendary ad agency that created the wonderful body of work for Apple, used to say, "What have you gained from wearing a $500 shirt, a $150 tie, $1,500 loafers, and a $7,000 suit? You're well dressed, certainly. But does it improve the person inside those clothes? Does it make your work any more valuable?"

A $500 shirt would have appalled my dad. Spending for the sake of spending or flaunting money made him downright angry. The concepts he instilled in me were work hard, earn a good living, and spend your money wisely. For him, spending wisely was the education he gave my sister and me. He never had a mid-life crisis that entailed a red Porsche convertible or a high roller's junket to Vegas.

I inherited his conservative money genes. I guess that's why I've never looked at Apollo as my personal ATM. It's probably why there's no yellow Lamborghini in my driveway, either.

You can do better than conspicuous consumption with your treasure. Draw what you need for a comfortable living. That's fair.

Invest as much as you can back in the business. Think of it this way: That business is the goose that produces the golden eggs. You want to keep the goose very healthy so it lives a long life and produces many more golden eggs for you.

I've heard people say, "The company doesn't need any money invested back into it. It's fine the way it is."

Possibly. But I'd suggest that almost every company could better fund research and development. At Apollo, for the last three years, we've reinvested a good percentage of gross sales back into research and development. Products and services continue to evolve at a faster and faster rate. We've invested heavily because we want to stay at the cutting edge of what's happening. You don't have to invest heavily if that's not in the cards, but invest something. This is one of those cases where if you're not making an effort, you're falling behind.

If you're in a customer service business, you probably need to invest more in marketing. Granted, most service businesses see marketing as an expense, not an investment, and begrudge every dollar spent. However, this is your connection to the customer. If you're not talking to your customers in the right places—Internet, social media, mass media—your competitors are.

Don't be a fair-weather marketer, either, spending money when times are good and being quick to stop if there's a downturn. Commit to a plan and stick with it. Cutting marketing in a market downturn is conventional thinking. Sound thinking says to start spending because when the market comes back, and it always does, your company's name is going to be one your customers are hearing.

Training is another often overlooked investment. I know at Apollo, we've benefited from executive coaching at the managerial level and from relationship development for the folks on the front line. We view training as a continuing expense. One training session will not generate the improvement you're looking for. Ongoing training creates the expertise that breeds esprit de corps and customer satisfaction.

And finally, there is no better place to reinvest money than in your people. You might be surprised at the return that investment produces. By paying your employees a little more than your competitors would, you create loyalty and positive feeling. That "little more" you're paying will more than pay for itself with less turnover and lower recruiting and training costs. Add employee recognition to the mix, and you could cut your turnover to zero. This is what will make you the employer of choice. You've used your wallet where most companies only use their mouths. You've shown that you value your employees, which will pay off for you in countless ways large and small.

LOOK AHEAD

❏ Consider making two timelines. Use the first to plot things as you foresee them happening. Use the second to plot how things might change if you make better use of your time.

❏ List your talents. List the talents that would be beneficial to you at work. Do you have an aptitude for some of the talents on this list of work talents? Could self-study help you become more talented in those areas?

❏ How important is money to you? In a column, list all the things you'd like to have and put dollar values next to those items. In a second column, list all the things you have that money can't buy. Compare the two lists and see where more money will truly make you happier.

Four-Dimensional Leadership

Up until now, we've been talking about pulling your organization forward—a task that will require your sharpened leadership skills.

But business is only one of four areas where those newly honed leadership skills can foster a purposeful life.

The four areas are: personal, family, business, and community.

I was first exposed to four-dimensional leadership at the EO Leadership Academy. I was immediately captivated by the concept and tried to put it into practice.

It's harder than you might think. In fact, after three years, it's still a work in progress for me. I want to share it with you because I've found as I work at holistic leadership, it makes me stronger in each individual area.

Why do I say this is still a work in progress? I believe holistic leadership is something you never quite master. I thought I was getting really good at it, but my mentor at EO brought me right back down to earth, saying, "You're not even operating at 50 percent capacity."

What? How could that be?

I was putting in hundred-hour weeks. I was a banshee at the office. You couldn't find anybody who worked harder.

And that was the problem.

I was using 100 percent of my business capacity but only 10 percent of my personal capacity, 10 percent of my family capacity, and a woeful 5 percent of my community capacity.

"Grasshopper," my mentor intoned, "you will not be fully four-dimensional until you are at 100 percent in all four areas." My problem, I quickly learned, was the way I'd organized my life.

I wanted to be a success at Apollo and gave it everything I had. I didn't hold anything back. What I failed to understand as I worked long into the night, every night, was that I was giving the company 100 percent and letting everything else fend for itself.

When I was rowing, I was eating right, exercising, taking care of myself physically. Once I stopped rowing, I lost my personal discipline. I ate too much. I drank too much. I started smoking heavily. I partied way too hearty. Before I knew it, my weight had ballooned to 250 pounds. I felt like a whale. I rationalized I needed to do all that because of how hard I was working. You've got to blow off steam, right?

In reality, I knew what I was doing to myself wasn't good. And my wife, in her own quiet way, tried to get me to change my habits.

But it wasn't until I was exposed to four-dimensional leadership that it all came into focus. Here I was, a guy who thought of himself as a leader, who wasn't a leader of *himself*.

The thought of how I had failed myself, of how I was so wrong in my actions, was truly humbling. It caused me to step back, say whoa, and think about how I wanted to conduct myself as a *person*.

I immediately lost 60 pounds, quit smoking, and cut back the drinking and partying. I've been asked if that was hard to give up, if I felt deprived of those pleasures. The answer is no.

Three mornings a week I'm at the gym before dawn; two other mornings I do Pilates. I'm back at the house in time to take my wife coffee as she's waking up.

PERSONAL

You see, **personal** is all about the concept of personal responsibility (PR). I'll confess I wasn't invested in that concept, but as I thought more about it, I realized how important this concept is. I also realized I wasn't the only one who wasn't being personally responsible. PR wasn't happening at any level in our society.

The president says Congress is to blame. Congress says the president isn't leading. Democrats blame Republicans. Republicans blame Democrats. Washington's a hot mess.

CEOs negotiate their golden parachutes before they ever start work. At the office, it's always the other person's job, the other person's problem, and the other person's fault.

Parents say the schools are failing their children. The schools say there's no discipline at home. Kids aren't worried about grades, they're worried about whether they can bring their cell phones to school and what kind of messages they can get away with on T-shirts. Meanwhile, test scores plummet. Our science scores are like twenty-seventh in the world. I think maybe we're behind New Zealand.

At home, you don't like what your spouse is doing; your spouse points the finger back at you. Maybe counseling can arbitrate. If that fails, you wouldn't be the first divorce on the block. The kids? It's too much work to wean them away from video games and texting their friends. Why bother? Let the schools instill discipline.

How did we get to be like this? We caved. We took the easy way. It's easier to blame someone or something than it is to fess up, take responsibility, and do the right thing.

Personal responsibility says you take complete responsibility for your actions. That's everything you do—not just when it's convenient.

I knew a CEO who was a hard worker, treated his people well, was a good family man with three small children, and coached little league. If you met him, you'd say, "Wow, what a great guy." Except . . . a couple of times a year he'd go to "business meetings" in Vegas. Once he was there, he gave himself over to the dark side—drinking, carousing, hitting the strip clubs, and gambling. It was as if he thought he should be able to take a vacation from personal responsibility.

It doesn't work that way. You don't get a pass on doing the right thing. If you're going to try to score a 100 percent on personal leadership, you've got to be in the program all the time.

To get me going in the right direction, my mentor taught me to prepare for the day. Instead of jumping out of bed, skimming the morning paper, and making a fast dash into the office, he had me do three things. I use my morning time like this:

1. **Ten minutes of thinking great thoughts:** I think about people who are adding value in the world, things that make a difference, things that turned out better than anyone expected because someone took the time to care. Little things. Big things. Great things. They're all positive things, and they put you in a positive mood.

2. **Ten minutes of reading:** No, not the morning paper, or worse, some tabloid from the supermarket. Invest in a business book that broadens your thinking, develops a talent, or expands your mastery of an area. I was never a reader growing up, but I have gained so much from the books I've read, I've become an avid reader. These days, I inhale books. I can't get enough.

3. **Ten minutes of writing:** You see the progression: ten minutes of your good thoughts, ten minutes of learning, now you're ready to put your learning, your thoughts, your hopes on paper. I believe in this so much that I have my management team journaling. Going back and rereading what I've written, I can see my own personal growth. If you had told me I'd gain this much insight by writing things down, I'd have told you that you were crazy. Crazy, yeah, like a fox.

Listening

So now I'm exercising, I'm thinking, I'm reading, I'm journaling. You'd think I'd be well on my way to that 100 percent on personal leadership. In fact, I was expecting my mentor to give me the executive equivalent of an Atta boy. Instead, he pointed to another key area of leadership—listening.

A lot of people think dieting is hard. To me, it's not. You know what you have to do: take in fewer calories than you use. Losing weight is really a matter of having the will to succeed. Well, I have plenty of will. And I have 60 fewer pounds to prove it.

Listening, unlike dieting, is far more undefined. I don't quite know how to do it properly, when to do it, or when I've done it enough.

I know I'm supposed to listen to understand, rather than listen to reply. But when you're a type A personality, it's hard to listen to reply, much less listen to understand. I want to jump in immediately and provide the answer; to heck with listening.

No. No. No.

Listening, I've learned, is a skill one must master. I've seen its value on those rare occasions where I've kept my mouth shut long enough to let someone else share a finished thought.

One of my management team came to talk to me about a personal problem. Because it was personal not business, I wasn't all about jumping in immediately with the answer. I let him talk and I practiced active listening. When he was finished, he got a smile on his face and said, "Thanks for listening. In talking it through, I see what I have to do. You've helped me a lot."

I didn't help him. He helped me. It was a validation of how important listening is to all four dimensions of leadership.

Personal leadership is an individual journey. No one can tell you what's right for you. I've learned that the more you reflect on it, the more you gaze into your soul, the more in tune you will be with determining the right journey for you.

FAMILY

In many ways, personal and family are so close they could be inter-twined. If you're not good to yourself, you're not going to be good to your family.

That was certainly the case with me. During the period where I was putting in hundred-hour weeks at Apollo, I was married and a father to two small boys. I never made family a priority. Consequently, my wife was constantly annoyed at me for never being home, for not paying attention to her, and my sons didn't know me.

One of the low points came when my wife, who is a reporter, was covering an important court case for MSNBC. She was on national television providing expert commentary. Me? I didn't see it. I was so tired from work I fell asleep on the sofa.

This was an important moment in her life, and I wasn't there for her. I will always regret that. I wasn't a leader to my family. I realized I couldn't work 24/7 and ignore my family.

Unfortunately, you can't just snap your fingers and make it right. You have to work at it every day. But I'm proud to say I can see the rich rewards that making an effort provides. My wife and I are happy again. And that feels so good. I'm doing all sorts of things with my boys who are now seven and nine years old. Both are playing soccer. I'll go to their games and practices. When there's an out-of-town match for one of my sons, he and I will make it a father-and-son road trip. We'll stay at a hotel and spend a lot of time talking. I love hearing each boy talk about his life. The more I hear, the more I realize how fast they are growing up and how close I came to missing all the wonderment of it.

I can't emphasis this enough. Don't wait. Don't spend the remainder of your life saying, "Gee, I wish I'd figured this out sooner." Make magic with your family now.

We're fortunate that we have a small cottage on a lake in Canada. There's no TV. No video games. No email. Just blue water, crisp air, and unbelievable peace and quiet.

Well, quiet until we get the jet skis out, and then, over the sound of motors, you hear the wonderful sounds of children's laughter. For us, Canada is magic time.

Whether it's at a vacation destination or just sitting around the kitchen table, that time together is so important. I find it's the only time when listening isn't hard for me. I just soak in all the boys' chatter. As I listen, I find I have opportunities to guide the boys just by asking them simple questions: "Your friend shouldn't have done that, should he?" "What did you learn from that?" "What's the right thing to do in that case?"

As they answer, I can see the wheels turning in their heads as they think it through and come up with the answer themselves.

These are little things that are big things. To me, this is family leadership of the best kind. I don't know whether my mentor would score it 100 percent, but it sure feels like it is.

BUSINESS

I've found that because my personal and family leadership improved, it has made my business leadership better. This goes back to that concept of balance—of not being 100 percent in one area and 10 percent in the others. I'm convinced that if you're more "centered" in your personal and family lives, you have a base from which to show more business leadership. This base, this reservoir of strength, makes a huge difference. With things I might have gone ballistic on before, I find I'm more controlled, more interested in resolution than fireworks.

We recently had a member of the management team roll out a new company initiative. Because this had to do with compensation, I would have liked him to have given each employee a written explanation of the new policy so that it would have been clearly understood by all. This management team member chose to do it verbally.

Of course, everyone heard what he said just a little bit differently. Here's a simplification of what happened: The manager said, "Apple." One employee said to another, "Apple? It should have been orange." That employee passed it along as, "It's apples now, but it's going to be oranges soon." The next employee passed it along as, "It's going to be oranges, but you know they'd really like it to be plums." That employee passed it along as, "I heard we're moving to plums." That employee passed it along with a sneer as, "Our new compensation plan is nothing but prunes."

Undoubtedly, you've had something like this happen at your workplace, and you know the damage miscommunications like this can do.

I could have yelled and screamed. But to me this was a leadership moment, a teachable moment. The manager and I discussed why he chose verbal communication. I listened closely. He shared good reasons why he'd communicated the new policy verbally. But with the clarity of hindsight, he realized that he'd made a mistake and had already come up with a plan of action to correct the situation.

I have never been prouder. He'd failed, taken responsibility, and moved to right the ship. You can't ask for more than that.

My leadership contribution was giving him the room to fail and allowing him the space to craft a solution. That's incredibly difficult to do. You want to do the leading rather than be the leader.

Business leadership isn't about you doing. It's about you being the leader. It's not about how many hours you work or what institutional knowledge you possess. It's about judgment. You have to be a good steward and display the kind of judgment that guides the organization on a purposeful path.

Being a leader requires two other traits—fairness and evenness.

Fairness

Let's take fairness first. It's easy to treat a manager you like or who is responsible for a moneymaking portion of the business a bit better than you treat other managers.

I had a friend who owned his own company. One of his managers had been his friend back in high school. He'd even been best man at my friend's wedding. The two had lunch together almost every day. Occasionally, my friend might have had lunch with one of his other managers, but those occurrences were few and far between. The other managers resented the special treatment the owner gave his long-time friend, but worse than that, they got all caught up in wondering what was going on at those lunches. Were the other managers being talked about? Were the two of them plotting something?

My friend never realized what chaos he was creating. He was just having lunch with a buddy. In all fairness to fairness, he should have known better. Once the unfairness genie is out of its bottle, it's hard to get it back inside.

Business leadership is about treating everyone equally and making each person feel important.

Evenness

Evenness is even more insidious than fairness. If you've ever worked for someone who's moody, then you've experienced the problem of evenness. The moody boss loves you one minute and hates you the next. Who knows what triggers those swings. All you know is that you're never quite sure what kind of reception you'll receive. And is it ever demoralizing to go to the boss with a good idea only to have it ridiculed because she's in one of her bad moods.

For the employees, it becomes a game. They pass the word to stay away. If things look good, they pounce to get what they want approved before the mood darkens. Good businesses don't run well in spits and drabs like this. They require a smooth pathway, and that nice, flat pathway starts with you.

As you move from doing the leading to being the leader, you should see your organization step up. Instead of doing all the pushing, you're giving your employees the positive power of Pull. Evenness and Pull fit together like two sides of a coin.

COMMUNITY

The fourth dimension of leadership is **community**. And right now you may be thinking, okay, I'm spending less time at the office, but I'm spending more time on me, more time at home with my wife and kids—there are only so many hours in the day—how is there time for community leadership?

Again, the answer is balance. Community moves you into a different realm in which you have the opportunity to grow and expand.

For over fifteen years, Apollo has been involved with the local arm of Habitat for Humanity. My dad got that involvement going. He was impressed, as am I, with how the organization operates. This isn't a give-you-something-for-free kind of organization. To be the recipient of a Habitat for Humanity home, you must invest five hundred hours of sweat equity and assume ongoing financial responsibility for the home's care and upkeep.

Habitat helps people help themselves.

That's a sorely lacking skill right now. And I think that's indicative of where we are as a culture. Growing up, I thought our country encouraged people to give more than they took. Today, I think it's gone the other way. We seem to have lost some of that community spirit. I don't see enough people stepping up to make an impact and make their communities better places. They're simply too absorbed in their own lives.

When I say community, that community could be a neighborhood, trade organization, historical society, beautification club, nonprofit, or arts organization. There are so many diverse communities deserving of your time that the list could be endless.

Giving some of your time to the community of your choice is a start. I recently joined the Habitat for Humanity board. Apollo, that year, had donated over 1,000 hours of community service and raised more than $10,000 in funding. Joining the board seemed to be the next step in assisting the organization.

Habitat's concept of helping people help themselves epitomizes community leadership. I can't say enough good things about what they're doing. This coming year, they'll build twenty houses. Twenty families will have the opportunity to invest themselves in changing their lives for the better. That's what I love about Habitat. They enable people to be successful. They reward the kinds of behavior—sweat equity and financial responsibility—that should be encouraged.

Earlier, I said giving of your time was a start. Certainly, Habitat takes community leadership a step further by giving considerably more than they take. But there's still another step that needs to be taken. To my knowledge, there isn't an organization devoted to holistically teaching the concept of leadership. There should be. This is far too important an area to be overlooked.

The idea first dawned on me during a conversation with my dad, right before the holidays. We were in the car, and he mentioned that Apollo would be sponsoring a needy family. I'm sure you're familiar with this program. Individuals and businesses are recruited to put together baskets of food and toys for distribution to the less fortunate. It's a good program. Still, I wanted the program to do more. I was reminded of the saying, attributed to Confucius: "Give a man a fish and you feed him for a day; teach a man to fish and you feed him for a lifetime."

I know there are organizations that Band-Aid problems, but where are the organizations that give families the skills to lead themselves out of those problems? I know social entrepreneurism like this is incredibly difficult, but where are the people stepping up to give it a shot? Few people have the fortitude to take on a challenge like this. Oh, they'll contribute money. But they don't know what to do beyond that. How do you pull past this?

The fisherman thought stayed stuck in my head. I wondered, *What if there was an organization that, through education and skill development, taught people to fish for themselves? An organization that gave people the tools to contribute as opposed to just receiving? An organization that taught you skills for free but required you to pay it forward three times?*

In honor of the thought that inspired it, I called it "The Fisherman's Fund."

At this point, it's still conceptual. Every day, as I talk to more people about it, it moves a little closer to become a functioning entity.

Here's the vision I've been sharing: The Fisherman's Fund would empower those who were less fortunate to fish for themselves. It would be based on four-dimensional leadership and strive to develop leadership qualities in all four of the areas. The training would be offered at no cost, but there would be a requirement that the participant pay it forward three times over. Why have this requirement? It's simple. Things that are perceived as "free" are sometimes thought to have little value. Cost creates accountability. With The Fisherman's Fund, pay it forward is the cost of entry into the program. The program itself would be divided into the four areas with initial content and discussion focusing on:

Personal

- Learning skills: What skill sets do you need in order to be successful? What do you need to invest in yourself to be a better person? How can you apply these new skills to being a leader?

- Goal setting: How do you set goals? How do you hold yourself personally accountable for your actions? What are your goals for one year? Three years? Five years?

- Communications skills: How can you be more articulate? How can you become a more active listener?

Family

- Spouse: How can you be more attentive and nurturing to your spouse? How can your spouse realize his or her hopes and dreams?

- Children: How can you develop positive parenting skills? How can you be a role model and help your children grow to be responsible adults?

- Parents and siblings: How can you show your support to the members of your extended family? Are there any steps you can take to stay in the know about their lives and concerns?

Business

- Stewardship: How can you run a more purposeful business? What are your priorities within the company? What are your responsibilities to the company, to yourself, and to your employees?

- Business basics: What are the skills you need to make your business more profitable? What are the skills you need to make it a more nurturing workplace? How can you make the company both people and profit directed?

Community

- Involvement: How can you take an active role in a

community? What are your obligations? How should you set goals for yourself in terms of making a difference?

- Pay it forward: How do you use what you've learned to empower other community members? How can you become a mentor to them?

Obviously, there's much more that needs to be done to make The Fisherman's Fund a reality. My hope is that the idea will attract support from a cross section of people who have done well in life. If these people will invest their time, talent, and treasure in the project, I'm confident we can make it not only a reality but also a tool that will enable real and lasting social change.

Before we leave the topic of four-dimensional leadership, however, I feel I have an obligation to warn you. There's shrapnel that comes from four-dimensional leadership. I got hit. You might, too.

Here's what happens. To learn, to experience something new, you have to leave your comfort zone. That transition between what was comfortable and what will be comfortable is scary. Everything you thought you knew starts to look wrong. Your head trash really starts doing a number on you. Those who are a tad weak in the knees will fold faster than a cheap card table chair. To grow, you have to embrace that discomfort and work at it until all the shades of gray change back to black and white.

Seeing things in black and white again usually means you've reached a new comfort zone. Luxuriate in it for just a moment before you jump back into discomfort. Because continuing to grow means you have to stay uncomfortable. The good news is the more you do it, the more natural it becomes.

Shrapnel? No problem. You've grown invincible.

LOOK AHEAD

Personal

❏ Take an inventory of how you feel about yourself. What are your strong points? What are the points you'd like to improve?

❏ Create a personal goal sheet. Set one-year, three-year, and five-year goals. What will it take for you to reach these goals? Once you have a list, prioritize it, and hold yourself accountable with due dates.

❏ Commit to starting your day differently. Spend ten minutes on thinking great thoughts, ten minutes on reading, and ten minutes on writing.

❏ Expand your horizons. Begin reading things that stimulate your mind and imagination or cause you to stretch and expand your reach.

Family

❏ Rate yourself as a spouse and as a parent. What are the things you're doing well? Where are the areas you need to make improvement?

❏ Are you helping your spouse to realize his or her hopes and dreams? If not, why not? What's standing in your way? Eliminate any barriers.

❏ Are you and your spouse spending time alone on a regular basis? Consider a date night. You may think that sounds corny, but it's great fun and will bring the two of you closer together.

❏ What are you doing with your children? Are you making one-on-one time for them with you? What activities can the two of you do together? My boys and I are about to take golf lessons together. Seems like a sport where we can spend time together now and far into the future.

❏ Are you making memories? Day-to-day demands are relentless. Don't let them keep you from making memories that you'll share and enjoy your entire life.

Business

❏ How can you shift from doing leadership to being a leader? If you had made that shift, what recent events might have gone better?

❏ Spend a day as a listener. Remember: It's not your job to have the first word or the last word. Just listen. See if you gain a better understanding of those with whom you interact.

❏ Review how fair you are. We all believe we're fair, but is that really the case? Make a list of who you favor and why. Make a second list of those you don't favor and why. What can you do to apply fairness overall?

Community

❑ What are the communities to which you'd be willing to contribute your time, talent, and treasure? Why? How can you contribute more than you take?

❑ Is there an idea you have to make a community better? Write it down. That's the first step to making it a reality. Who can you involve to help you make your idea a reality?

The Power of Pull Redux

I hear you thinking, *Jamie, all this is well and good, but if I do all this stuff you've talked about, can you guarantee it will improve my business?*

I wish I could. I wish I could give you the winning lottery numbers, too.

But I can say this. I'm confident that if you harness the positive power of Pull, it will improve your business. I base that firmly on what it has done for Apollo. When I bought the business from my dad, Apollo had thirty employees. We're now at seventy-five and hiring as fast as we can. In a down economy, where many in the trades were struggling, we've enjoyed double-digit growth every year I've been running the company. I think that's a testament to the power of Pull.

Pull Theory is a mindset. It's a toolbox of improvements that shifts a traditional business out of fourth place and takes it all the way to first place. In describing Pull Theory, we've talked about a lot of different things. Here's a recap of the pieces I've shared with you.

WHAT SUCCESS FEELS LIKE

I've always had a clear vision of what success would be like for Apollo. Pull Theory helped us achieve it in a number of ways. Monetary success is the easiest to measure, and we've certainly achieved that. We've been successful at things that are harder to measure, too. We have a more motivated workforce. You can feel a sense of energy in the office; we're solving challenges and meeting customer expectations. This is a fun place to come to work. That, to me, is a telling measure of success. It all starts with that vision of success. Make sure you've captured your vision of success. Write it down on paper; fill a whiteboard. How you do it isn't important. Doing it is.

SEE YOUR FUTURE

Visualization isn't only for athletes and super big businesses. You can use this powerful tool to preview your future. Use it to paint a picture of where you want to be in one year, three years, and five years. Use it to help you see how improvement initiatives might generate more business. Visualize on your own or involve your staff.

PARADOX OF LEADERSHIP

With the positive power of Pull driving the organization, I can step away if I need to. I'm confident that I have talented people motivated and monetized to excel in my absence. If one of them should fail, the organization will pull together and pick up the slack until the situation is resolved. As a leader, you can't be afraid to let your people fail. Failing is a normal part of growth. As a toddler, you failed a bunch of times before you could walk. As a child, you fell off your bike before you learned to ride. Business is no different. Failure is a part of learning. If you're smart, you'll structure the organization to contain the damage. At Apollo, we've done that. I can go on a vacation or attend a conference and know the business will keep humming while I'm out of the office.

CAPITAL T, LITTLE T TALENT

In our world, it's hard to attract Capital T talent. Recognizing that, we've made great strides in identifying and hiring Capital T talent in training. Our management team is young, aggressive, and likes to make things happen. Our frontline techs are a different breed than their predecessors. They're no longer wrench jockeys. They're better with diagnostic tools and communication with the customer. We've also hired Capital T women who want to rejoin the workforce after leaving to have a family.

Look at the needs of your workforce and see if the energy of Capital T's in training might give your organization a lift. Root out all Little t's and Little t's in Capital T disguise. Getting rid of the underperformers and adding overachievers will swing the pendulum to the positive.

SQUIRREL VERSUS DOG

We now have people with the right abilities in the right places. This is essential to having everyone pulling his or her weight. That old saw about an organization only being as good as its weakest link is so true. You have to have all the links—all the oars—strong and pulling together. Apollo has that now. One part of the organization doesn't slow another part down. Don't settle for dogs if there are squirrels or thoroughbreds to be had.

MAKING THE CIRCLES CONCENTRIC

Good talent expects to be respected. Part of that respect is giving the person the authority for his or her area of responsibility. You can visualize this with two circles labeled Authority and Responsibility. If the two circles are standing side by side, responsibility and authority are separated. When they overlap, the employee has authority for that portion of his or her job. When the Authority and Responsibility circles are concentric—essentially one on top of the other—the employee has authority commensurate with responsibility.

MINDSET AND MOTIVATION

With the right people in the right places, we were able to fine-tune mindset and motivation. I believe we've done a good job of kicking head trash to the curb and replacing it with a feeling that we still haven't realized our full potential. The lesson I learned from my rowing coach is with me every day: "You won't win if you don't *believe* you can win." We've become believers at Apollo. Get rid of your head trash and make yours an organization of believers.

THE COMMUNICATIONS CONUNDRUM

We're all adults at Apollo. We tell it like it is, and we do it face-to-face. No one is second-guessing what someone says or what something means. That's the way it needs to be. Life's too short and business moves too fast to play games. I understand the reasoning for political correctness, but too often that gets in the way of helping someone. Sometimes a hard truth is what's needed.

THREE TO GO

We're always looking to improve. So there are three improvement initiatives in play at any given time. While change can be a distraction, these initiatives—many of them focused on process and systems—have institutionalized values and methods of doing business in a way that has deepened the culture of our company. Institutionalize work improvement at your shop. Always keep improving the business. That way you'll stay current with the market and attractive to employees.

BIRTH TO DEATH: THE BUSINESS LIFE CYCLE

Once your business hits maturity, you need to find a way to keep from moving to the next phase—decline. One way is by allowing your employees to "pull" the organization forward. Another way is to add an additional service line that may restart growth.

OVERWHELMED

Transitional change breeds stress. In fact, even the thought of change can be stressful. Often that stress can cause inertia that is difficult to overcome. Breaking change into small chunks makes it less stressful and easier for people to move forward. Ignore those within your company who are negative about your efforts. Remember that you can't please everyone. As a good steward, what you are doing should be what is in the best interest of the company.

R (RELATIONSHIPS) + OR – V (VALUE) = $ (PROFIT)

A friend and I were talking about company assets and, until I cut him off, he was talking about his truck fleet. Really? Trucks? Relationships are the asset that counts. If you can build deep, enduring relationships, you've created value, and your business will prosper. Everything at Apollo is structured to strengthen those relationships. We're honored that many of our customers have been with us ten, twelve, and fifteen years. Have your organization pulling on the customer's behalf, and I believe you'll enjoy that kind of loyalty, too.

THE ELEPHANT IN THE ROOM

It's crucial that you have a good handle on your financial position. If you are in a negative cash flow situation, make corrections. Your biggest expense is salaries, and while it's never easy to let people go, it's better to rightsize your business than continue to bleed red ink. Take a realistic look at your sales ability. If you find it lacking, don't hesitate to hire a business development professional or invest in sales training for you and your staff. Keep in mind those two good rules of thumb for well-run businesses: 50-25-25—50 percent of gross income for salaries, 25 percent for expenses, and 25 percent to business reserves/profit. The second idea is third/third/third— as an owner spend one-third of your time on operations, one-third with customers, and one-third on business development.

OVERCOACHING OR UNDERCOACHING

We've cut the number of meetings we hold and made the meetings we do have more efficient. Give your people the room and time to do what you've asked of them. Don't hold too many meeting, but don't hold too few, either. Make sure you're involved at key points in the process. Use a scorecard, or Management by Walking Around is another way to keep your finger on the pulse of your business.

HIGHS AND LOWS

We celebrate our wins as a group. At Apollo, this has built great esprit de corps. I have no doubt celebrating the highs will have a positive effect in your organization, too. When we experience lows, we use them as a teaching opportunity. You'll get big credit for handling negative situations positively.

INSIDE AND OUTSIDE

Inside things are all the actions you take to create knowledgeable, motivated employees in an efficient and effective workplace. Outside things are the marketing actions you take to connect with customers and potential customers. Marketing is an enigma to most traditional businesses, and that's a shame because good marketing is simply creating a conversation with your customers. The best way to do that is to create a profile of your best customers and learn when, where, and how they would like to receive communication. By getting to know your best customers, you also get to know those customers who are most likely to buy from you. Reaching these new potential customers is a vital step in keeping your business busy, active, and engaged.

THREE RIGHTS FOR SUCCESS

Marketing boils down to saying the *right thing*, at the *right time*, in the *right place*. Remember, this is a zero sum game. If you don't get all three right, your efforts are meaningless. Viewing communications from the customer's standpoint will help you be successful. Help the customer understand why you are his or her best choice.

THE GAME CHANGER

Thanks to the Internet, you can play with the big boys. The web gives you a long-form information source that, if used properly, can create a professional image, showcase capabilities, and give the customer an easy to way to schedule appointments or get a quote. The web is a game changer. Don't fail to take advantage of this valuable tool.

RINGS AROUND THE BULL'S-EYE

Working with your customer profile, you may learn that your customers would be very receptive to an additional service offering from you. Think of this as a target with the bull's-eye representing your core service and your customer. As you add rings, make sure you stay true to both your core service offering and your customer base.

TIME, TALENT, AND TREASURE

Each new day you are given is a miracle. Figure out how much runway you have left and make a list of all the things you want to accomplish. Don't waste time. Once it's gone, it's gone. Don't waste your talents. Apply the ones you have and develop new talents that will serve you well. Spend your treasure on the things that matter: personal, family, business, and community.

The Apollo of today isn't the company I bought from my dad. Oh, the name's the same and the logo hasn't changed, but the company has been reconceptualized to make it more customer-centric and growth oriented. With our core heating and cooling business thriving, we expanded our business both vertically and horizontally. Vertically we made further improvements to our service model and extended our service area into additional neighborhoods. Horizontally we added plumbing, which is a natural fit with HVAC, and it has grown into a mature service offering. With the success of plumbing, we've explored adding more services and will offer those in the near future.

When I look at the company, I see a young, motivated staff; best practices utilized in every business unit; and growth that is both vertical and horizontal. I see a very bright future.

I'd like to say I did all that. I didn't. Every employee at Apollo deserves the credit because they're pulling the company forward. Each and every one of them is making *their* company, Apollo, a success.

The Apollo story is gaining traction. I've been speaking to business groups, mostly luncheon or company meetings, on "How to Grow a Traditional Business." Naturally, I think it's a good talk, and companies seem to take a lot away from it.

For me, this is the best kind of pay it forward. Folks come up to me and say:

> "It was so good to hear you. I've got those same problems, and getting the company moving seemed like an insurmountable task."

> "I never thought about push vs. pull, but pull makes sense. We'll make the switch."

> "I agree with you on pay-for-performance. It could make a huge difference at our company."

"I got more from listening to you than I did from a bunch of fancy-schmancy business books."

As I say in my talks, you can do it. You can make a traditional business into a growth business. Yeah, you'll be rowing against the current. But once you build a little momentum, those oars will glide through the water, and you'll feel the boat picking up speed. You'll be on your way. The positive power of Pull will carry you to success.

Every company is different. But I believe, like a good food recipe, the power of Pull gives you all the ingredients for success. How you measure the ingredients and put them in the mix is up to you. The same is true for applying heat. Some people want things to simmer. Some people bring things to a boil as quickly as possible.

What Pull Theory does is give you an overarching theme you can use to easily let the entire organization understand what's expected. I hope you'll put it to work in your organization and, when you do, I hope you'll share the results with me. I'm confident you'll be the next Pull Theory success story.

About the Author

Jamie Gerdsen is a business owner, an innovator, and an entrepreneurial thought leader. His milieu is not high tech or digital; it's in the traditional—and definitely unsexy—world of small local business: home heating, air conditioning, and plumbing. Innovation is not often associated with Main Street businesses. But contractors, repair services, HVAC providers, dry cleaners, and the like are the backbone of commercial life in cities and towns across America, as well as the essential drivers of the national economy.

In 2010, Jamie took over Apollo Heating and Air Conditioning, his family's century-old Cincinnati heating, air conditioning, and plumbing company. There, he has put to use his ideas on how small enterprises can innovate to help boost revenues and profits. In 2005 he introduced the proprietary Apollo University program to train his employee service staff for North American Technician Excellence certification. He also introduced a performance-based structure (unusual in most small businesses) and forged highly collaborative business partnerships with his suppliers and vendors.

By seeking innovation amidst the mundane, Jamie's relentless insistence on positive change has paid off handsomely in strong returns, five prestigious and consecutive customer service awards, recognition as an entrepreneur, and multiple awards from HVAC manufacturers. In 2009 and 2011, Jamie was a finalist for the Ernst & Young Entrepreneur of the Year, and Apollo was a finalist in a local competition of Best Places to Work multiple times due to its focus on the holistic well-being of the employee.

Even before joining Apollo, Jamie displayed a restless desire that typifies the entrepreneurial mind. After graduating from Boston University, which he attended on an athletic scholarship, Jamie was part of a team that took public a seventy-five-employee startup, raising more than $330 million in investor capital for the market launch.

In Cincinnati, Jamie founded the Fisherman's Foundation to encourage innovation and leadership in traditional businesses. He is also involved in a variety of community organizations, including Habitat for Humanity, the Goering Center for Family and Private Business, Cincinnati Preservation Association, and Leadership Cincinnati. In 2011, he was named to the city's Forty Under 40 class, an honor that designates emerging business leaders. In 2012, he was the winner of the Next Generation Leader from the Northern Kentucky Chamber of Commerce. A letter of recommendation for that award described Jamie as "one of the most inquisitive individuals I have ever met," who operates with the "core values of respect, passion, accountability, family, trust, and integrity."

Jamie is a widely respected business speaker and published author. Among his work are "The Push Pull Theory of Leadership," published in *Octane*, a publication of the Entrepreneur's Organization, and "10 Ways to Keep Current Customers Coming Back," in *HVACR Business.*

It is perhaps illustrative of his business mindset that Jamie won seven national championships in rowing—a sport in which individual exertion must be seamlessly linked in a group effort, with each oar pulling in the same direction. This is a formula for success in rowing, business, and certainly in life.

Find out more about Jamie Gerdsen at www.fishermansfoundation.org.

Index

overview, 33–35, 197
for sales in times of trouble, 107
celebrating the highs, 121–23, 201
CEO
  chain of command in absence of,
    57–58
  controlling everything, 47–49,
    112–13
  delivering truth as favorable
    learning experience, 71
  dividing your time, 109
  exit strategy, 88
  and financial problems, 104
  and Friday afternoon complainers,
    93
  as good shepherd, 123
  and hiring, 38
  improvement plan involvement, 94,
    95–96
  management by walking around,
    114–16
  and marketing, 150–51
  matching responsibility with
    authority, 49–50, 51, 198
  role in creating employer of choice
    status, 43–46
  and speed of change, 94, 96
  See also four-dimensional leadership
chain of command, 57–58
challenges for employees, 55–56, 58
coaching
  for Capital T's in training, 128–29
  judgment necessary for, 184
  management by walking around,
    114–16
  and meetings, 112–14, 116
  mentoring, 25, 31
  new management team, 122
  overview, 111–12, 201
  problems associated with, 112–13
  See also communication; leadership
    coaching
commission sales, 2, 7–8
commitment to marketing, 173

communication
  with customers and suppliers about
    financial problems, 106
  employee personal development and
    communications training,
    98, 99
  face-to-face, 69–70, 72
  on highs and lows, 119–23, 201
  honest, 70–73
  of installers with customers, 97
  learning about, 189
  listening, 180–81, 182
  management by walking around,
    114–16
  meetings, 112–14, 116
  miscommunication jumble, 183–84
  overview, 69, 74, 199
  sales as form of, 107–8
  of service tech with customers, 80,
    99–100
community leadership, 121–22, 186–89,
  190–91, 193–94
competitive advantage, visualization
  as, 12
competitor's brand messages, 140
competitor's customer profiles, 136
complementary service offerings
  Apollo's plumbing service, 161–62,
    204
  expense and reward, 127–28
  overview, 87, 88, 203
Confucius, 188
confusion from communication, 112,
  113
consumer goods companies, 8–9
control
  CEO controlling everything, 47–49,
    112–13
  dealing with employees' need for,
    55–58
  employees' need for, 54–55
  as paradox of leadership, 31, 51, 113,
    196–97
conventional thinking, 3, 92

Follow My Blog Posts

If you enjoyed this book, I invite you to follow me on my blog at:
www.fishermansfoundation.org

Speaking Engagements

I enjoy speaking to business groups large and small. To determine my open speaking dates, please contact me. I can be reached on the web at: www.fishermansfoundation.org or by phone at 513-404-2718.